Jesus

Model of Manhood

Jesus

Model of Manhood

Sewell Hall

Jesus, Model of Manhood

Published by Mount Bethel Publishing,
P.O. Box 123, Port Murray, NJ 07865,
www.MountBethelPublishing.com

ISBN: 978-0-9850059-7-9

Cover Design: - Bethany Hubartt,

Printed in the United States of America

Dedicated to

my many young friends

who, in their youth,

remember their Creator

and

seek first the Kingdom of God

and His righteousness.

Contents

Table of Contents

INTRODUCTION

S ome years ago, we had a young boy in the church who was an avid Braves baseball fan. He also liked to play baseball, and when he got up to bat you knew immediately who his baseball hero was. You could tell by his posture, by the way he held his bat, went into his stride, and swung.

We all tend to become like our heroes. It is not necessarily that we intend it. It is not that we consciously imitate them. Usually, it is simply an unconscious reflection of the qualities of those we admire.

Who are your heroes?

Whoever they are, you will be eager to know all you can learn about them. You will want to be in the company of friends who share your admiration for them, and you will want to exchange information about them. As they become more and more dominant in your thinking, you will find yourself becoming more and more like them. This is not good if your heroes are not good role models.

Many years ago, in a church where I was preaching, a young man came before the church to make a confession. He admitted that he had been obsessed with the feats of a popular football star and, as suggested above, he had gone to every source of information available to learn everything he could about him. Much of what he learned about his hero's lifestyle off the field, however, could only be classified as sinful. The young Christian was confessing that he had allowed himself to be drawn into some of those sins by his mere admiration of his athletic hero. Wisely, he was expressing his determination to change heroes.

God has not left us without heroes to be studied, admired and even imitated. In the Old Testament, He revealed Himself as a model for Israel in a demonstration of His awesome qualities at Mount Sinai. Then God exhorted the Israelites, "You shall therefore be holy, for I am holy." But "so terrifying was the sight that Moses said, "I am exceedingly afraid and trembling" (Hebrews 12:21).

The God of Sinai would be hard to imitate or even to see as one's hero. Man needed to see what God would be like in human form. To provide such a model, God, called the Word, "became flesh and dwelt among us, and we beheld His glory, the glory as of the only begotten of the Father, full of grace and truth" (John 1:14). God in the flesh we know as Jesus. When He called His disciples, His challenge was, "Follow Me" (Matthew 4:19).

Numerous passages from the New Testament also challenge us to follow Him.

"For I have given you an example, that you should do as I have done to you" (John 14:15).

"A new commandment I give to you, that you love one another; as I have loved you, that you also love one another" (John 13:34).

Speaking of God: "For whom He foreknew, He also predestined to be conformed to the image of His Son, that He might be the firstborn among many brethren" (Romans 8:29).

"He who says he abides in Him ought himself also to walk just as He walked" (1 John 2:6).

I ask again, who is your Number One hero? If you are a Christian, it must be Jesus. "For to this you were called, that you should follow His steps" (1 Peter 2:21).

I believe there are many young men who would say that Jesus is their hero. Some, however, seem to have little inclination to study His life. They seem to think they can know what Jesus would do by their own imagination. Jesus often said and did things that seemed strange to worldly observers. Long ago, two Proverbs used the same words to warn, "There is a way that seems right to a man, but its end is the way of death" (Proverbs 14:12 and 16:25). To be sure that we follow "His steps" we must study the writings of those who actually lived with Him for three years of His life on earth.

This little book is intended to help you in your study of some of the facets of the life of Jesus. In the beginning, however, let me insist that neither this book nor any other can

substitute for your study of the writings of those who were
with Him while He lived on earth. Speaking of Jesus as "the
Word," the apostle John wrote,

> What was from the beginning, what we have heard,
> what we have seen with our eyes, what we have looked
> at and touched with our hands, concerning the Word of
> Life...we proclaim to you also, so that you too may have
> fellowship with us; and indeed our fellowship is with
> the Father, and with His Son Jesus Christ (1 John 1:1,3
> NASB).

"But we all, with unveiled face, beholding as in a mirror the
glory of the Lord, are being transformed into the same image
from glory to glory, just as by the Spirit of the Lord" (2
Corinthians 3:18).

Chapter 1

His Life's Goal

"For I have come down from heaven, not to do My own will, but the will of Him who sent Me" (John 6:38).

When I was a small boy, we lived on a street near a fire station. Very often, the fire truck would come down our street on the way to a fire. As soon as I heard the siren, I ran out to see it pass by. I loved the clanging of the bell and the roar of the engine as it got closer. It must have been one of the older machines in the city, for it often backfired and I could see sparks flying from underneath, but that made it even more exciting. As I observed the fireman driving the vehicle or the men hanging on to the side, I was sure that I wanted to be a fireman when I grew up.

The next place we lived was in a town dominated by the railroad. The big steam locomotives were even more exciting than the fire truck. Instead of sparks, they belched clouds of steam and shook the ground like the rumble of thunder. I wanted to be as near the tracks as my parents would allow when one of those mighty engines roared by. We even had a family friend who drove one, and I was sure that one day I wanted to be a locomotive engineer like Mr. Porter.

If space travel had begun, I probably would have dreamed next of being an astronaut.

Like most boys, my early ambitions involved excitement and personal pleasure. Goals change, however, as reality sets in. We begin to realize that not all of us are physically or mentally qualified for some of those more exciting occupations. We begin to think more about making a living and the occupations that will put food on our tables and clothes on our backs. As we have families, their needs must also be met. A few individuals, however, go beyond the idea of meeting their own needs to seek ways of unselfishly serving others. And that was true of Jesus.

Jesus

Jesus was the only person in all history who lived before He was physically conceived. The writer of the gospel of John calls Him "the *Word.*"

In the beginning was the Word, and the Word was with God, and the Word was God. He was in the beginning with God. All things were made through Him, and without Him nothing was made that was made. (John 1:1-3)

He made His plans for what He would be and what He would do on earth before He even came into the world as a babe. His Spirit was in the Old Testament prophets as they prophesied of His coming (1 Peter 1:10-11). His Spirit enabled them to foretell many things that He would do even before He was born.

Any plan Jesus made for His earthly existence would mean incredible sacrifices. In heaven, He possessed all the wisdom, power and glory of God. Any earthly existence, even as the richest, most powerful king or emperor, would demand a step down that would be more dramatic than any we can imagine. But He did not choose earthly royalty or wealth for Himself on earth. The Spirit describes the level to which He stooped in Philippians 2:6-8.

> Being in the form of God, [He] did not consider it robbery to be equal with God, but made Himself of no reputation, taking the form of a bondservant, and coming in the likeness of men. And being found in appearance as a man, He humbled Himself and became obedient to the point of death, even the death of the cross.

His Goal

His Spirit in Isaiah predicted that He would have a body. "'The Lord Himself will give you a sign: Behold, the virgin shall conceive and bear a Son, and shall call His name Immanuel" (Isaiah 7:14).

The Psalmist, a thousand years before He was born, identified the purpose for that body.

Sacrifice and offering You did not desire,
But **a body You have prepared for Me**.

...

Then I said, "**Behold, I have come—**
In the volume of the book it is written of Me—
To do Your will, O God" (Psalm 40:6-8 as quoted in
Hebrews 10:5,7 Emphasis mine S.H.)

The purpose of His body was to provide the fleshly structure
in which He could do God's will and the instrument with
which it could be done. During His lifetime, He identified this
as the purpose of His coming. "For I have come down from
heaven, not to do My own will, but the will of Him who sent
Me" (John 6:38).

The cross was not something that happened to Him
unexpectedly. He knew it would be His experience on earth
(Revelation 13:8). Yet He came to earth anyway. He had a
mission to accomplish regardless of the cost. "The Son of
Man did not come to be served but to serve, and to give His
life a ransom for many" (Matthew 20:28).

And in what area of man's needs did He come to serve?
In medicine? In education? In government? In science?
Outstanding success in any one of these fields would have
served mankind and doubtless made Him popular and
possibly rich. He tells us, instead, what service He intended to
render. "The Son of Man has come to seek and to save that
which was lost" (Luke 19:10). This was His goal because it
was God's goal for Him.

For God so loved the world that He gave His only
begotten Son, that whoever believes in Him should not
perish but have everlasting life. For God did not send His
Son into the world to condemn the world, but that the
world through Him might be saved (John 3:16-17).

Planning Our Own Lives

Those two things said about Jesus in the Old Testament are
just as true of us.

The Source of our Bodies: God made our bodies and gave
them to us. We must confess that we had no part in it. God's
creation of our bodies is described in Psalm 139.

You formed my inward parts;
You covered me in my mother's womb.
I will praise You, for I am fearfully and wonderfully made;
Marvelous are Your works,
And that my soul knows very well.
My frame was not hidden from You,
When I was made in secret,
And skillfully wrought in the lowest parts of the earth.
Your eyes saw my substance, being yet unformed.
And in Your book they all were written,
The days fashioned for me,
When as yet there were none of them. (Psalm 139:13-17)

Not only did God form our bodies, but when we became
Christians, He redeemed them from the slavery of sin

and gave us "the gift of the Holy Spirit" (Acts 2:38).
Consequently, "Do you not know that your body is the
temple of the Holy Spirit who is in you, whom you have from
God, and you are not your own? For you were bought at a
price" (1 Corinthians 6:19-20).

The Purpose of Our Bodies: Our bodies were not given
to us that we might wring from them as much pleasure as
possible. They were not given to provide us with the means of
gaining fame through sports or entertainment, nor were they
designed to enable us to gain riches. God certainly allows us to
use them for legitimate activities intended to sustain and enrich
our lives, but that is not the purpose for which they were given.

God has revealed the purpose for our bodies. "Therefore
glorify God in your body and in your spirit, which are God's" (1
Corinthians 6:20). We are as obligated to do this as Jesus was.

We may not be called upon to sacrifice our bodies on a cross
as Jesus did, but we are commanded to give them as living
sacrifices. "I beseech you therefore, brethren, by the mercies
of God, that you present your bodies a living sacrifice,
holy, acceptable to God, which is your reasonable service"
(Romans 12:1). There is probably no better exposition of this
verse than the familiar hymn of Frances R. Havergal.

> Take my life and let it be
> Consecrated, Lord, to Thee.
> Take my moments and my days,
> Let them flow in endless praise.

Take my hands and let them move
At the impulse of Thy love.
Take my feet and let them be
Swift and beautiful for Thee.

Take my voice and let me sing,
Always, only for my King.
Take my lips and let them be
Filled with messages from Thee.

Take my silver and my gold,
Not a mite would I withhold.
Take my intellect and use
Every power as Thou shalt choose.

Take my will and make it Thine,
It shall be no longer mine.
Take my heart, it is Thine own,
It shall be Thy royal throne.

This purpose—to do God's will in your life—is the first and essential decision you must make if you would follow in the footsteps of Jesus. Have you made this the supreme goal of your life?

Questions

1. What were some of your life's ambitions when you were a small boy?

2. Why do our childish goals change?

3. Why was Jesus able to set His life's goals, even before He was born?

4. How is it that we can learn about the goals that He had even before He was born?

5. What proves that His coming to earth was not a selfish choice?

6. What does the Hebrews quotation of Psalm 40 reveal as the goal of Jesus in coming to earth?

7. What was God's will for Him (John 3:16-17)?

8. What two facts about the bodies of Christians prove that God owns them?

   a.

   b.

9. What, then, is the purpose of our bodies?

10. List some ways that we can present our bodies as a "living sacrifices."

Chapter 2

Jesus, Model of Manhood

His Heavenly Father

"Did you not know that I must be about My Father's business?" (Luke 2:49)

athers generally dominated the families described in the Bible. The first dispensation of God's will to man is called the Patriarchal age, but the word *patriarch* means father. If God had a message for a family during that period, He delivered it to the father. Abraham, Isaac and Jacob are known especially as the three patriarchs. They were fathers of God's chosen people.

"The husband is head of the wife…" (Ephesians 5:23). He is also responsible for the training and discipline of the children (Ephesians 6:4).

Mary's husband Joseph must have been a good father. Surely God would not have chosen Mary to be the mother of His Son if Joseph had not been qualified to be a good father, for she was espoused to Joseph and espousal in that culture meant that marriage was almost inevitable. When Jesus was born, several actions were required by the law of God and Joseph was careful to see that everything was done exactly "as it is written, in the law of the Lord" (Luke 2:23,24).

Joseph made several significant sacrifices of personal freedom to protect Jesus. Though he went ahead and married Mary as God instructed, he did not have marital relations with her "till she had brought forth her firstborn Son" (Matthew 1:25). He fled with his family to Egypt to protect young Jesus from Herod's sword. Then, continuing to protect Him, he returned to Nazareth rather than to Bethlehem when he was warned by God in a dream.

After Jesus was brought to live in Nazareth, "His parents went to Jerusalem every year at the Feast of the Passover. And when He was twelve years old, they went up to Jerusalem according to the custom of the feast." (Luke 2:41). This, too, is commendable in Joseph. He included Jesus in this spiritual pilgrimage. Joseph is one of the few men in the Bible about whom nothing negative is said. He might well be studied as the model of a good father. However, on that visit to Jerusalem another and superior Father was identified in the life of Jesus.

God: If the Bible records any failure of Mary and Joseph as parents of Jesus, it was on that same visit to Jerusalem. History indicates that most devout Jews went by the temple as the last stop before leaving the city. One can imagine Joseph and Mary doing this with Jesus in their company.

And anyone familiar with 12-year-old boys can also imagine
that Jesus could become so absorbed with the activities
in the temple courts that He did not notice His parents
leaving. They must have been so accustomed to His good
behavior that they just assumed that He was with other family
members in the large company that often traveled together.
And it was only when they stopped for the night that they
realized He was not among them.

It took another day for them to return to Jerusalem and
only on the third day could they begin their search. And
where should they find Him but where they had left him—in
the temple courts, "sitting in the midst of the teachers,
both listening to them and asking them questions. And all
who heard Him were astonished at His understanding and
answers" (Luke 2:46-47).

One would suppose that His parents would simply sigh in
relief and rejoice in what they were seeing and hearing. But
their anxiety was not so easily relieved, and Mary interrupted
to say, "Son, why have You done this to us? Look, Your
father and I have sought You anxiously" (Luke 2:48).

The answer of Jesus must have surprised them. He said,
"Why did you seek Me? Did you not know that I must
be about My Father's business?" (verse 49.) Notice that Mary
had said, "**Your** father," obviously referring to Joseph. Jesus
responded by speaking of "**My** Father," obviously referring
to God. God now took precedence over Joseph as the Father
of Jesus.

Application

A definite change takes place when a child becomes a youth. As a child, his life is dominated by his parents. God intends that this be so. Ideally, he is obedient to parents because he respects their age, their experience and their love, believing that they love and desire the best for him. But this is not always the case. Sometimes a boy may obey simply because he seeks their approval or their reward. Or, it may be only because he knows his parents are bigger than he is and he fears the punishment they can apply. If he disobeys them, he may have difficulty sleeping because he thinks he is "in trouble." Next morning, however, he has forgotten his fears and he awakes ready to take on the world.

After the change, however, a youth becomes aware of a guilt that does not vanish with the morning light. Often, he turns inward and there is a definite change of personality.

The most important change is an awareness of a change in relationship with parents. Parents are still an important influence in his life, but he becomes aware of a higher authority. A sense of right and wrong develops that is independent of what parents have taught him. He may now find it difficult to go to sleep at night because his conscience is condemning him for things his parents have never mentioned. He may even feel guilty about things that he knows his parents approve. He may not be able to identify God as the authority he senses, but he knows there is one, whether he can identify it or not.

The young man who has been brought up by godly parents knows Who that authority is. He knows it is the God Who made him, his Creator. He has been taught that the Bible is God's message to teach him how God wants him to live. He knows that to "fear God and keep His commandments" is what life is all about (Ecclesiastes 12:13). And he knows that "God, who at various times and in various ways spoke in time past to the fathers by the prophets, has in these last days spoken to us by *His* Son" (Hebrews 1:1-2).

At this point in life, a young man needs to make the one greatest decision of life. Shall I live my life doing the will of God or doing my own will?

At the age of twelve, Jesus consciously confirmed the great decision He had made before His birth: "Did you not know that I must be about My Father's business?" (Luke 2:49).

There is, however, an interesting follow-up verse. Even after that decision, "He went down with them and came to Nazareth, and was subject to them" (Luke 2:51).

Why was He subject to His parents even after recognizing the Heavenly Father as the supreme authority? Well, the answer is that as long as He was still in the home of His earthly father, He was about His Heavenly Father's "business" when He was obedient to His earthly parents. The fifth of the Ten Commandments was: "Honor your father and your mother, that your days may be long upon the land which the LORD your God is giving you" (Exodus 20:12). This was often repeated, both in the Old and New Testaments. Jesus referred to it (Matthew 15:3-6) and the Holy Spirit, through Paul, reinforces it for Christians (Ephesians 6:1-3). Those words were not written primarily for little children to memorize, but for mature individuals to understand and obey.

What About Baptism?

Sin is a violation of God's will. When a young child disobeys parents, he is not sinning. He does not yet know God as the supreme authority. He may feel a sense of guilt, but it is more related to parents than to God. It is only when the sense of guilt that is unrelated to parents develops that he becomes a sinner.

I believe that many children are baptized too early. They may do it to please parents. They may react to a challenge from other children: "I'll go if you will." Some may be eager to become adults and think of baptism and observing the Lord's Supper as symbols of maturity. Others may be moved by fear of the consequences of some big mistake they have made, even of a bad report card. It may be fear stirred by some sermon that graphically described the torments of Hell, and they don't want to go there. None of these, however, is a reason for baptism.

Baptism is "for remission of sins" (Acts 2:38, 22:16). One has no sins to be remitted or washed away until he has gone past violating the will of parents and violated God's will for him.

Baptism is putting to death and burying an old life of sin and being "raised to walk in newness of life" (Romans 6:2-3). It is a mature commitment to "put on Christ" (Galatians 3:27). Children are not mature enough to make such a lifetime commitment.

What about the baptism of Jesus?

Why was Jesus not baptized until He was thirty (Luke 3:23)? The simple answer is that it was not a command of God until "John came baptizing in the wilderness and preaching a baptism of repentance for the remission of sins" (Mark 1:4). That was 18 years after His visit to the temple when He was 12. It was the first opportunity He had to be baptized after committing Himself to His "Father's business."

When John the Baptist was commissioned to begin baptizing, "Jesus came from Nazareth of Galilee, and was baptized by John in the Jordan" (John 1:9). Jesus had no sins to be remitted but, as He explained, "It is fitting for us to fulfill all righteousness." (Matthew 3:15).

When a young man becomes a sinner by consciously violating the will of the Heavenly Father (not just parents), he should then be baptized for the remission of those sins and "to fulfill all righteousness."

Questions

1. What is the position of a father in the family?

2. What three facts prove that Joseph was a good step-father?

a.

b.

c.

3. Where did Joseph and Mary find Jesus after they had lost Him?

4. What was He doing?

5. How did Jesus indicate awareness of another father than Joseph?

6. What are some physical changes that take place in a boy about the age of 12?

7. What are some changes that occur in his conscience and awareness of guilt?

8. Did the fact that Jesus was aware of a heavenly Father keep him from obeying His parents?

9. What are some wrong reasons that may motivate children to want to be baptized?

11.   What is sin?

12.   When is one old enough to be baptized?

13.   Why was Jesus not baptized until He was 30?

Chapter 3

His Increasing in Wisdom and Stature

"And Jesus increased in wisdom and stature" (Luke 2:52).

T he few words of Luke 2:52 are all that is recorded of the eighteen years between our Lord's visit to the temple at the age of twelve and His baptism at the age of thirty. However, it is a complete description of the wholesome development that should be seen in every young person.

Increase in Wisdom

The early Christian writer, Clement of Alexandria, stated that the noun translated *wisdom* meant "knowledge of divine and human matters."

Much of the knowledge of "human matters" is gained by observation. Jesus was evidently a keen observer of things around Him. His teaching is filled with allusions to what He would have seen in nature. Apparently, He had observed and identified eagles, doves, ravens, and sparrows as well as hens with their chicks. He had seen sheep following the shepherd as well as lambs going astray. He had watched the farmer sowing his seed and seen the resulting development of the blade into fully formed ears. He knew the qualities of the mustard seed and the lilies of the field. He knew the flash of lightning in the sky and the meaning of weather signs in the clouds.

His knowledge of nature was just the beginning. He was equally aware of the least noticeable characteristics of home life in Nazareth. He had seen a woman hide a little leaven in a lump of dough and seen her light a candle to seek for a lost coin. He knew the practices of those in the marketplace who cheated customers with a small measuring cup. All of this, and more, found its way into His wonderfully picturesque teaching.

From some source He learned languages. His reading of the scripture in the synagogue is proof of His knowledge of the Hebrew language. His direct quotations from the Greek translation of the Old Testament and His conversations with Pilate and other foreigners are evidence that He spoke Greek. This was in addition to His constant use of the Syriac or Aramaic language which was the common language of Galilee.

His knowledge of divine matters was obtained from scripture. When He was only 12, the teachers of the Old Testament law in Jerusalem "who heard Him were astonished at His

understanding and answers" (Luke 2:47). And as He entered
His ministry, His knowledge of God's word was always
superior to that of the Scribes and Pharisees who tried to trap
Him with their devious questions.

A young person who would increase "in wisdom" as Jesus did
will give careful attention to the world around him and to the
study of God's word.

Diligence in studying subjects that are taught in school is
also valuable as long as one is aware of the fact that there is
a "knowledge that is falsely so called" (1 Timothy 6:20-21).
When Jesus lived, there were numerous philosophies being
taught in the schools of which there is not a trace in the
teaching of Jesus. "The fear of the Lord is the beginning of
knowledge" (Proverbs 1:7). Any "knowledge" that does not
have its roots in the fear of the Lord is without foundation.
Much of what is taught in schools today ignores God and
assumes evolution as the origin of our existence. The Spirit,
through Paul, warns against such "knowledge."

Just as there are two kinds of knowledge, there are two kinds of
wisdom. James, the brother of Jesus, describes a devilish wisdom.

> If you have bitter envy and self-seeking in your
> hearts, do not boast and lie against the truth. This
> wisdom does not descend from above, but is earthly,
> sensual, demonic. For if you have bitter envy and self-
> seeking in your hearts, do not boast and lie against
> the truth. This wisdom does not descend from above,

but is earthly, sensual, demonic. For where envy and self-seeking exist, confusion and every evil thing are there. (James 3:14-16).

The world calls a person wise who knows how to serve his own selfish interests and get to the top regardless of how many people he may hurt on his way up. Not only are the streets of many neighborhoods cursed by such selfish wisdom, but so are many offices and too many homes. Indeed, as James stated it, "where envy and self-seeking exist, confusion and every evil thing are there."

This was not the wisdom in which Jesus increased!

James also describes a wisdom that is from above. "The wisdom that is from above is first pure, then peaceable, gentle, willing to yield, full of mercy and good fruits, without partiality and without hypocrisy" (James 3:17). No words could be chosen that would better describe Jesus. He was "first pure, then peaceable, gentle, willing to yield, full of mercy and good fruits, without partiality and without hypocrisy." He was heavenly wisdom personified. Proverbs describe this wisdom also. "The fear of the LORD IS THE BEGINNING OF WISDOM, and the knowledge of the Holy One is understanding" (Proverbs 9:10).

A life of wisdom is not simply knowing what is wise, but it is doing what we know is wise. Most of us on occasions have known what was wise, but for some thrill or gamble or immediate pleasure we have done what we knew was foolish. And often we have suffered the consequences.

Solomon is an interesting study. He is described in scripture as a wise man. The Proverbs and the conclusion of Ecclesiastes prove that he knew what was heavenly wise. But all too often he practiced worldly wisdom rather than practicing "the wisdom that is from above." He did what seemed to be to his immediate advantage. Sometimes it seemed wise in the short run. but in the long run the result was disgrace for him and disaster for his family and the nation. As someone has well said, "It is always right to do right, and always wrong to do wrong."

Increase in Stature

What did Jesus look like? The many paintings that have circulated through the years all differ depending on the culture and imagination of the artist. If that is the source of your ideas, you probably think of Him as a frail and weak looking person. Actually, the passage quoted from Luke tells us all we can know about the appearance of his physical body. It seems to be saying that He had a normal development into a normally strong body.

Glimpses we have of Jesus in the New Testament seem to demand a strong body. His work as a carpenter demanded it. His grueling schedule of work, punctuated by whole nights spent in prayer, required it. The picture of Him, twice cleansing the temple, making a whip of cords and driving out sellers of oxen and sheep and doves with their merchandise, and overturning the tables of the money changers (John 2:14-15) is hardly the picture of a frail and delicate weakling. All of this is climaxed in His strength to survive the abuse that He suffered even before the crucifixion. We are told that many criminals died under the scourging that He endured.

If Jesus "increased in stature" it is evident that He avoided ingesting chemicals that would stunt His growth. A question which almost any doctor will ask a new patient is, "Have you ever smoked or used alcohol." The long-lasting ill effects of such popular habits are well-known.

He must have eaten a healthy diet. He was poor, and the diet of the poor is often healthier than the rich foods served up to the rich.

Doubtless He exercised. Of course, He did not have the electronic games, cell phones, computers, TV's that keep so many teen-agers indoors, out of the sunshine and fresh air. Did He play sports for recreation? He mentions the games that children played (Luke 7:32), but by the time our text describes Him, He probably did not have very much time for play.

In Mark 6:3, Jesus is called a carpenter. The life of a carpenter in those days was a hard life. They did not have the labor-saving tools that carpenters use today. It has been said that if a carpenter was working in wood, he had to go into the woods, chop the trees and dress the lumber before beginning his construction. Some authorities say that the word carpenter included stonework which would require even more physical exercise. Doubtless, such labor would produce a strong man.

Application

Far more important than the appearance of the body of
Jesus was His attitude toward it. The very fact that so little is
said about His appearance is evidence that He was basically
unconcerned about that. We have already seen that He saw
His body as a gift from God to make it possible for Him
to do the will of God. This being true, we can be sure that
He would be concerned to keep it in good condition for
that purpose. It would always remain His servant, never His
master. More of this later.

Questions

1. What indicates that young Jesus was a keen observer of
His surroundings?

2. What languages did Jesus know and use?

3. From what source did Jesus learn divine knowledge?

4. What is the beginning point of true knowledge?

> What is some popular "knowledge" that does not
> begin there?

5. What are two kinds of wisdom identified in the book of
James?

6. What words does James use to describe worldly wisdom?

7. What words does James use to describe "wisdom from above"?

8. Which words best describe Jesus?
Which best describe you?

9. What are some implications that Jesus had a strong body?

10. What do you see in the records of the life of Jesus about the importance of one's physical appearance?

11. From what we learned in Chapter 1 about what Jesus considered the purpose of His body, why do you think He would take care of it?

If we understand the purpose of a Christian's body, how will this affect the care we take of our own bodies?

Discussion Question

Was Solomon wise or unwise?

Chapter 4

His Increasing Favor with God and Men

"And Jesus increased in...favor with God and men" (Luke 2:52).

In Favor with God: In view of what we have seen thus far in the life of Jesus, we are prepared for the fact that He increased in favor with God.

Absolute sinlessness in the life of Jesus was essential to His mission, which was to offer Himself as a sacrifice without blemish for the sins of the world. Perhaps we can imagine the satisfaction with which God saw Jesus pass through those difficult adolescent years and on into His 20's with not one sin on His record.

When Jesus was 30 (Luke 3:23), He went to the Jordan to be baptized by John. There He received the approval that He deserved.

> When He had been baptized, Jesus came up immediately from the water; and behold, the heavens were opened to

Him, and He saw the Spirit of God descending like a dove and alighting upon Him. And suddenly a voice came from heaven, saying, "This is My beloved Son, in whom I am well pleased" (Matthew 3:16-17).

To be well-pleasing to God is the most important achievement possible. What trophy or medal (even gold) or plaque or crown or letter or prize or award of any kind can compare to pleasing God? A Golden Globe Award or a Heisman trophy or a Homecoming Crown can never compare. Yet, how diligently some of us train and perform in hope of attaining such human rewards, and how little we think of that most significant one!

The apostle Paul wrote,

> But with me it is a very small thing that I should be judged by you or by a human court. In fact, I do not even judge myself. For I know of nothing against myself, yet I am not justified by this; but He who judges me is the Lord. Therefore judge nothing before the time, until the Lord comes, who will both bring to light the hidden things of darkness and reveal the counsels of the hearts. Then each one's praise will come from God (1 Corinthians 4:3-5).

Thank God, we do not have to live a sinless life as Jesus did in order to gain God's favor. Regardless of how hard we may have tried, all of us have sinned and by our sin we have lost God's approval. But, because Jesus lived a sinless life and gave it as a sacrifice on the cross,

You, who once were alienated and enemies in your mind by wicked works, yet now He has reconciled in the body of His flesh through death, to present you holy, and blameless, and above reproach in His sight— if indeed you continue in the faith, grounded and steadfast, and are not moved away from the hope of the gospel (Colossians 1:21-23).

Walking in the footsteps of Jesus does not mean that we will never sin, but it does require resisting sin and making God's approval the chief goal of our lives. Once we realize our sin, we will repent and ask God's forgiveness as David did.

Have mercy upon me, O God,
According to Your lovingkindness;
According to the multitude of Your tender mercies,
Blot out my transgressions.
Wash me thoroughly from my iniquity,
And cleanse me from my sin.

For I acknowledge my transgressions
And my sin is always before me.
Against You, You only, have I sinned,
And done this evil in Your sight—
Create in me a clean heart, O God,

And renew a steadfast spirit within me
The sacrifices of God are a broken spirit,
A broken and a contrite heart—
These, O God, You will not despise. (Psalm 51:1-4, 10, 17).

In Favor with Men

As we have seen, favor with God is by far more important than favor with men. However, favor with men is important. Otherwise, it would not be mentioned here.

Current thinking is that every person has a right to be whatever he wants to be and to do what he wants to do, and it is nobody else's business. "What other people think about me doesn't matter," they say. This is not the message of the Bible.

The same apostle Paul who wrote, "with me it is a very small thing that I should be judged by you or by a human court," also wrote concerning his use of funds, "avoiding this: that anyone should blame us in this lavish gift which is administered by us—providing honorable things, not only in the sight of the Lord, but also in the sight of men (2 Corinthians 8:20-21).

Our effectiveness in sharing the gospel depends to a great degree upon the respect people have for us. If they see us as self-centered and hypocritical, they will not likely listen. If they see in us sincerity, humility, pure motives, love and concern for others, their hearts will be open. These must have been the qualities that Jesus developed in His early years that commended Him to His neighbors.

Paul is an example of one who sacrificed his "right" to be what he wanted to be. He made himself a servant of all, and that meant doing what he could conscientiously do to please others rather than himself. He adapted his habits and practices to the culture of those he was trying to reach.

> For though I am free from all men, I have made myself
> a servant to all, that I might win the more; and to
> the Jews I became as a Jew, that I might win Jews; to
> those who are under the law, as under the law, that I
> might win those who are under the law; to those who
> are without law, as without law (not being without law
> toward God, but under law toward Christ), that I might
> win those who are without law; to the weak I became as
> weak, that I might win the weak. I have become all things
> to all men, that I might by all means save some. Now
> this I do for the gospel's sake, that I may be partaker of it
> with you. (1 Corinthians 9:19-23)

Giving up our own preferences and submitting, as a bondservant, to the preferences of others is not easy, but this is what Jesus had to do when He left heaven. In heaven He was God. On earth He was still God, but with the limitations manhood necessarily implies. "The Son of Man came not to be served but to serve, and to give his life as a ransom for many" (Matthew 20:28 ESV).

A Warning

Obtaining favor with men must never become our primary goal. We seek the favor of men only that we may please God and increase in His favor. We never compromise in our determination to please God.

There comes a time when we cannot please both God and men. Especially, as we grow older, having favor with men of the world and favor with God is usually impossible. James said it this way: "Do you not know that friendship with the world is enmity with God? Whoever therefore wants to be a friend of the world makes himself an enemy of God" (James 4:4).

This is one of the dangers in professional sports or entertainment. We become addicted to the fame and acclaim they provide. Then when it seems to be necessary to do something that violates our conscience in order to advance our career, we find it difficult to say, "No." So, one small step at a time we abandon our faith. Professional sports and entertainment are a spiritual graveyard for most young people. I have known many who began along that road, but seldom have I seen one survive.

Society may admire the nice little boy. But when he becomes mature and they realize that he has no fellowship with their unfruitful works of darkness but rather exposes them (Ephesians 5:11), they will turn against him.

After all, it was the men of Nazareth, in whose favor Jesus increased as a youth, who later tried to kill Him by throwing Him off a cliff (Luke 4:28-30).

Questions

1. Why was it necessary for Jesus to be sinless?

2. What testimony did God give to prove that Jesus pleased Him?

3. How does God's approval compare to winning a medal, trophy, or title among men?

4. Whose approval was Paul most concerned about receiving (1 Corinthians 4:3-5)?

5. Do we have to live a sinless life as Jesus did to be approved by God?　　Why or why not? (See 1 John 2:1-2)

6. Does the greater importance of God's approval mean that it does not matter what people think about us? Explain.

7. What was Paul's dual concern about how he handled money in his care (2 Corinthians 8:20-21)?

8. What accommodations did Paul make to increase his influence with those he taught?

9. What are some qualities that men approve that will increase our influence as we teach them?

10. What are some dangers in making the favor of men our goal?

11. What are some dangers in pursuing a career in sports or entertainment?

Chapter 5

His Temptations

"In all points tempted as we are, yet without sin" (Hebrews 4:15)

Since Adam and Eve, temptation has been the common experience of all mankind, including Jesus. In all things He had to be made like His brethren, that He might be a merciful and faithful High Priest in things pertaining to God, to make propitiation for the sins of the people. For in that He Himself has suffered, being tempted, He is able to aid those who are tempted (Hebrews 2:17-18).

But could Jesus have sinned? Apparently He could have; else He could not have been tempted. But He could also NOT sin, and He did not. And in this He is our great example.

The fact that Jesus was "tempted in all points as we are" does not mean that He was tempted with all the devices that Satan may use to tempt us. It does mean that Jesus was tempted through all the natural desires that we have. Someone has called them the desire for pleasure, for acquisition and for achievement.

When God created us, He gave us desires for things that we need for life, and He made it feel good to satisfy those desires. We need food, rest and warmth, and satisfying those needs is pleasant. Even sexual desires are given us to assure the continuation of the human race. But these must remain our servants and not be allowed to be masters that control us.

The desire for acquisition makes us desire a house and other necessities of life so that we do not have to depend on others. But when it causes us to want more than we need and causes us to steal or to be dishonest, it becomes a sin.

The desire to achieve encourages us to be successful in legitimate undertakings, but if it becomes an ambition that drives us to seek the praise of men rather than the approval of God, it becomes sinful.

Once these desires begin to control our lives, they are called lusts. So the apostle John warns. "All that is in the world—the lust of the flesh, the lust of the eyes, and the pride of life—is not of the Father but is of the world" (1 John 3:16). James described temptation in these words: "Each one is tempted when he is drawn away by his own desires and enticed. Then, when desire has conceived, it gives birth to sin; and sin, when it is full-grown, brings forth death" (James 1:14-15).

When Satan approached Adam and Eve, they had the desires God had given them, but not lusts. By the time he left them, however, their desires for pleasure, for acquisition and for achievement (to be like God) had been stirred to the point that their desires became their masters, and they violated the clear instructions that God had given them.

Satan undertook the same approach with Jesus, but it failed. Jesus resisted. He did not sin.

Jesus was Prepared

First, we have seen that Jesus considered that His body was created to make it possible for Him to do God's will. The first and foremost question regarding any proposal was, "Is this God's will?"

Furthermore, He was confident that the scriptures revealed God's will. So, the second question was, "What do the scriptures reveal to be God's will concerning this proposal?"

These two convictions, already formed in the mind of Jesus, determined His reactions to each temptation. And it is with these two convictions that we must face our own temptations if we would be as successful as He was.

The Temptations

The First Temptation was the temptation to turn the stones of the wilderness into bread. Due to His humanity, the desire was greatly increased by the fact that He had not eaten for forty days. "Afterward He was hungry" (Matthew 4:2). This would seem to be an understatement. But the question was not, "Was He hungry?"; but rather, "Is this God's will?".

There was no scripture specifically saying, "Thou shalt not turn stones to bread." But Jesus was not satisfied with this. One can almost imagine His thinking through the scriptures to see if there was any example of God's servants being in a position like the one He was facing. And, indeed, He remembered one. The children of Israel had set out from Egypt with a promise of God's care and had experienced a lack of bread. Moses later observed,

> So He humbled you, allowed you to hunger, and fed you with manna which you did not know nor did your fathers know, that He might make you know that man shall not live by bread alone; but man lives by every *word* that proceeds from the mouth of the LORD (Deuteronomy 8:3).

Jesus must have thought, "If they were to trust God and live by what He told them to do, that is what I must do." So, this became His answer to Satan. "It is written, 'Man shall not live by bread alone, but by every word that proceeds from the mouth of God'" (Matthew 4:4). In other words, "I have no word from God to prove that this is His will."

Our first question concerning any proposed action must be: "Is there a word from God that approves this action?"

The Second Temptation:

> Then the devil took Him up into the holy city, set Him on the pinnacle of the temple, and said to Him, "If You are the Son of God, throw Yourself down. For it is written: 'He

shall give His angels charge over you,' and, 'In *their* hands they shall bear you up, lest you dash your foot against a stone'" (Matthew 4:5-6).

The pinnacle of the temple was a place where huge crowds would be assembled. Seeing a man gently carried from that high point by angels and safely deposited on the temple courts would have created a sensation! It would have made Jesus into a celebrity. It might even have caused some witnesses to acknowledge Him as the Messiah! But was this God's plan? True, Satan even quoted scripture, but was that scripture actually instructing God's servants to take unnecessary risks to prove that God was with them? Somehow, it didn't sound right.

One of the first rules of good Bible interpretation is to consider all that God's word says on a subject. This is what Jesus did, and He remembered a verse that said "You shall not tempt the Lord your God" (Deuteronomy 6:16). Jumping from the pinnacle of the temple would be tempting God to see if He would keep His word. That verse did not specifically mention a jump from the temple pinnacle, but it is clearly **implied** that He should not do it. That was His answer to Satan. "It is written again, 'You shall not tempt the Lord your God'" (Matthew 4:7).

Third Temptation: Satan offered Jesus "all the kingdoms of the world and their glory" if He would only bow down and worship him. Jesus had come to establish a kingdom, but to obtain it by worshiping Satan, even once with nobody watching, would be an obvious violation of an **express command** in scripture: "You

shall worship the Lord your God and Him only you shall serve"
(Deuteronomy 6:20). This was the answer Jesus gave to Satan.

Lesson for Us

Satan tempts us by inflaming our God-given desires until they
become lusts and overpower our commitment to God. He
tempts us with the desires of the flesh, with our ambition for
the praise of men and with our desire for things. Just as Jesus
defeated Satan by His determination "to do God's will" and
by His conviction that God's will was contained in scripture,
we can do the same.

"But Satan quoted scripture." Yes, and so do many
of his agents. Peter warned that "untaught and
unstable *people* twist [the scriptures] to their own
destruction" (2 Peter 3:16). So, when any teacher advocates
anything, we must follow the example of the noble Bereans
who, even when they heard Paul preach, "searched the
Scriptures daily *to find out* whether these things were so"
(Acts 17:11). This is exactly what Jesus was doing as He
considered Satan's proposals.

Jesus was able to resist Satan's temptations and NOT sin.
It is also true that when we are tempted, we CAN sin, or
we can NOT sin. The choice is ours! "Therefore submit to
God. Resist the devil and he will flee from you" (James 4:7).
"For to this you were called, because Christ also suffered
for us, leaving us an example, that you should follow His
steps: Who committed no sin…" (2 Peter 2:21-22).

I have found the promise in 1 Corinthians 10:13 a great defense in times of temptation.

> No temptation has overtaken you except such as is common to man; but God is faithful, who will not allow you to be tempted beyond what you are able, but with the temptation will also make the way of escape, that you may be able to bear it.

This means, first, that others have been tempted just as I am, and they have resisted successfully. If they could, I can. Furthermore, just as God limited the extent to which Satan could tempt Job, He limits how Satan can tempt me. God knows that I can overcome this temptation or He would not allow Satan to use it! "God is faithful." He is watching out for me!

All of us have sinned. We have failed to resist temptation. We must never willingly submit to Satan, but when we realize that we have done so, all is not lost. If our heart is right, godly sorrow will lead us to repentance (2 Corinthians 7:10) and we will look to God for the grace He offers.

> My little children, these things I write to you, so that you may not sin. And if anyone sins, we have an Advocate with the Father, Jesus Christ the righteous. And He Himself is the propitiation for our sins, and not for ours only but also for the whole world (1 John 2:1-2).

Questions

1. How was Jesus "tempted in all points" as we are?

2. What are some good uses to be made of the desires that God has given us?

     a. Pleasure

     b. Acquisition

     c. Achievement

3. In what two ways can these beneficial desires be turned into sinful lusts?

     a.

     b.

4. How did Satan turn these desires in Adam and Eve into lusts leading to sin?

5. What two facts about Jesus prepared Him to resist the temptations?

6. Does the first temptation strike us as being sinful? Why would it have been a sin?

7. Why would it have been wrong for Jesus to jump from the

pinnacle of the temple?

8. Why would it have been wrong for Jesus to worship Satan, even once?

9. What three words did Jesus use in all of His rejections of Satan's temptations?

10. How can we follow the example of Jesus in preparing to resist Satan's temptations?

11. What are some lessons that you see in 1 Corinthians 10:13 that can help in time of temptation?

12. What must we do when we realize that we have sinned?

Discussion Question

What are some ways that Satan turns OUR God-given desires into lusts that lead to sin?

a. Pleasure

b. Acquisition

c. Achievement

Chapter 6

His Vocation

The Lord has annointed Me to preach good tidings..." (Isaiah 61:1)

Jesus was a carpenter. Justin Martyr, an early Christian, wrote, "He used, when He was among men, to work as a carpenter, making ploughs and yokes." A more recent writer says, "Jesus built the cottages of the villagers of Nazareth, constructed the wagons of the farmers, and mended perhaps the plaything of the child." Whether He engaged in these exact activities or not, He was most certainly identified as a carpenter by His neighbors in Nazareth (Mark 6:3).

Joseph apparently died sometime between the visit to Jerusalem when Jesus was twelve, and the beginning of His ministry eighteen years later. But before Joseph passed, he evidently accepted what was considered the duty of every Jewish father - to see that his son learned a trade. And that would explain the fact that Jesus was a carpenter as Joseph was.

But carpentry was not His vocation. The word *vocation* is from a Latin word that means "calling." One of the definitions of *vocation* is "A calling of an individual by God, especially for a religious career" (The American Heritage® Dictionary of the English Language, 5th Edition). Carpentry was something that He did to provide income so that He could pursue His vocation.

Jesus identified His vocation. "The Son of Man has come to seek and to save that which was lost" (Luke 19:9). This was the purpose for which God sent Him into the world, not to be a carpenter.

The Spirit of Christ through Isaiah had prophesied the method by which He would save the lost. "The Spirit of the Lord GOD *is* upon Me, Because the LORD has anointed Me to **preach** good tidings to the poor; He has sent Me to heal the brokenhearted, to proclaim liberty to the captives, and the opening of the prison to *those who are* bound" (Isaiah 61:1). (Emphasis mine S.H.}

Jesus might have formed a fan club by jumping off the pinnacle of the temple, as Satan suggested. Or He might have gained a kingdom by worshipping Satan; many kingdoms have been won that way. But Jesus was not interested in attracting large numbers of half-hearted followers. Rather, those who were to be saved by Him would be saved by being convinced that He was God's Son and by totally committing themselves to Him, regardless of the cost. Such faith would have to be strong enough that the believer would be willing to "deny himself, and take up his cross daily, and follow" Him (Luke 9:23).

Followers with such faith and commitment could only be gained by capturing their minds and changing their thinking; and this could only be accomplished by teaching. He said, "you shall know the truth, and the truth shall make you free" (John 8:32). Consequently, "Jesus went about all Galilee, teaching in their synagogues, preaching the gospel of the kingdom" (Matthew 4:23). His brothers did not understand His methods because they did not understand His mission (John 7:1-5).

When Jesus called His first disciples, He said, "Follow Me, and I will make you fishers of men" (Matthew 4:19). This was their new calling (vocation): to fish for men as Jesus was doing—by teaching. When He was leaving the earth to return to Heaven, He said to His disciples, "All authority has been given to Me in heaven and on earth. Go therefore and make disciples of all the nations, baptizing them in the name of the Father and of the Son and of the Holy Spirit, **teaching** them to observe all things that I have commanded you; and lo, I am with you always, *even* to the end of the age" (Matthew 28:18-20).

This means, then, that if we have been saved by the teaching of Jesus through those disciples, our calling (vocation) is to "observe all things that" He commanded them - to "make disciples" and to teach them. Paul instructed Timothy: "The things that you have heard from me among many witnesses, commit these to faithful men who will be able to teach others also" (2 Timothy 2:2).

Our Vocation

It is clear from the above that all of us who intend to be like Jesus must be teachers. "But you *are* a chosen generation, a royal priesthood, a holy nation, His own special people, that you may proclaim the praises of Him who called you out of darkness into His marvelous light" (1 Peter 2:9). The Hebrew writer chided his readers because "when by this time you ought to be teachers, you need *someone* to teach you again the first principles of the oracles of God" (Hebrews 5:12).

Being a teacher like Jesus does not mean that one must "find a preaching job" or even preach from a pulpit or teach a formal Bible class. Jesus was as much a teacher when He conversed alone with the Samaritan woman as when He was preaching in the synagogues. A person who does not accept each opportunity to speak about Jesus with individuals is hardly ready to preach to multitudes.

Being a teacher like Jesus does not mean that we must enroll in a seminary or Bible School to learn the Bible and learn how to preach. It is not wrong to learn the Bible from whatever source we can learn it, but it is not essential to enroll in a school. Paul was trained in such a school, but Jesus was not. We do not know all the ways that Jesus came to know the scriptures as He did, but it was not in the school where rabbis were expected to be trained. The villagers who called Him a carpenter "were astonished, saying, 'Where *did* this Man *get* these things? And what wisdom *is* this which is given to Him'" (Mark 6:2)?

Doubtless, His parents obeyed the instructions of
Deuteronomy 6:6-7:

> And these words which I command you today shall be in
> your heart. You shall teach them diligently to your children,
> and shall talk of them when you sit in your house, when
> you walk by the way, when you lie down, and when you
> rise up.

Furthermore, it was His custom to attend the synagogue on
the Sabbath (Luke 4:16). There He would hear the scriptures
read and discussed.

In addition, Jesus must have done much personal study which
prepared Him with knowledge far exceeding that of the
recognized Rabbis who had attended the schools. Some of
the greatest preachers of the gospel through the years have
received little training at home and none in a religious school.
They taught themselves the scriptures and took advantage
of opportunities the local church afforded for learning and
leading in worship.

Being a teacher like Jesus does not mean that we must avoid
all secular employment. Paul is an outstanding example of one
who supported himself and his companions, by tent making
when necessary. Aquila was also a tentmaker and Luke was
a physician. Even today, it is good for young men planning
to preach the gospel to learn a trade or occupation that they
can follow when support is not available for preaching. One
young man I knew was training to be a barber and another a

pharmacist because employment (even part-time) is available for such work most everywhere. Some of the greatest preachers and teachers I have known in my lifetime have supported themselves by engaging in another occupation. But their vocation was preaching and teaching the gospel. Everything else was intended to contribute to that calling.

It is not wrong to be supported by those we are teaching (Galatians 6:6). There is no record of another occupation being followed by Timothy or Titus or several other evangelists named in the New Testament. More to the point, perhaps, is the fact that Jesus left His carpentry when He began His major mission. No doubt there were good reasons for His waiting to the age of 30 to begin that mission, but from that point on He was supported by His followers, including some women (Luke 8:3). That period, however, was not an easy time for Him. On one occasion He said, "Foxes have holes and birds of the air have nests, but the Son of Man has nowhere to lay His head" (Luke 9:58).

One who would follow Jesus as a soul-winner should not expect to be popular or to have an easy life. Godliness is not a way of gain (1 Timothy 6:5). Soul-winning often involves sacrifice, whether we follow another occupation or not. Paul wrote to Timothy, "You therefore must endure hardship as a good soldier of Jesus Christ. No one engaged in warfare entangles himself with the affairs of this life, that he may please him who enlisted him as a soldier" (2 Timothy 2:3-4).

What do you see as your vocation in life?

Questions

1. Was Jesus a preacher or a carpenter?

2. What did God send Him to do in His lifetime (His vocation)?

3. How was He to accomplish His lifetime calling?

4. What did Jesus say He would make His early disciples to be (Matthew 4:19)?

5. If we are to do what Jesus instructed His apostles to do (Matthew 28:19-20), what will be our calling (our vocation)?

6. Does this mean that we must:

   a. Find a "preaching job"?

   b. Preach or teach publicly?

   c. Attend a preacher training school?

7. What are some likely ways that Jesus learned God's word?

8. Why is it good for any preacher to have back-up skills, even if he is supported by a church?

9. Is it wrong to be supported by those we teach?   How do you know?

10. What do you see as your vocation?

Chapter 7

His Synagogue Experience

*"And Jesus went about all Galilee, teaching in their synagogues,
preaching the gospel of the kingdom" (Matthew 4:23).*

When Jesus lived, there was a synagogue in almost every community in the Mediterranean world where there were ten devout Jewish families. The word *synagogue* at first meant "gathering" but it came to be used more often for a "gathering-place," especially a gathering place for Jewish worship.

Synagogues were apparently first formed when the temple had been destroyed and the Jews were isolated from Jerusalem during the Babylonian captivity. Devout Jews wanted to continue to worship God together, so they gathered each Sabbath to read the law, meditate on it and pray to God. Eventually they began to build simple buildings for this purpose. Even after their return from captivity and the rebuilding of the temple, they continued their Sabbath gathering in synagogues. There were many synagogues, even in Jerusalem.

Synagogue worship was much simpler than the elaborate
ceremonies of the temple. There were no sacrifices in the
synagogue, so ordained priests were not required. "Laymen"
could do the reading and teaching that were done there.
Volunteers were usually permitted to participate.

The synagogue offered important opportunities for devout
young men who wished to increase in the favor of God.
There were at least three advantages it offered:

1. It would be the best environment possible for such a
person to 'increase in the favor of [good] men." The best
people of the village gathered in the synagogue on the
Sabbath, and they were the kind of people who would
respect and encourage a young man who was trying to grow
spiritually. He might be ridiculed by worldly people, but he
would be praised by synagogue people.

2. It would be the place where a young man could learn about
God. Copies of God's law were extremely expensive, and
few families could afford even one book. But the synagogue
had copies and they were carefully preserved. James, the
Lord's brother, observed, "Moses has had throughout many
generations those who preach him in every city, being read in
the synagogues every Sabbath" (Acts 15:21).

3. Synagogue gatherings would also give him opportunity to
participate actively in the services, developing his talents in
public reading and speaking.

It is not surprising, then, to read that soon after Jesus began His personal ministry, "He came to Nazareth, where He had been brought up. And as His custom was, He went into the synagogue on the Sabbath day, and stood up to read" (Luke 4:16).

We would expect that this would be a pleasant and affectionate reunion with His old neighbors. And it did seem to begin that way. After He had read from Isaiah 61:1-2,

> Then He closed the book, and gave *it* back to the attendant and sat down. And the eyes of all who were in the synagogue were fixed on Him. And He began to say to them, "Today this Scripture is fulfilled in your hearing." So all bore witness to Him, and marveled at the gracious words which proceeded out of His mouth. And they said, "Is this not Joseph's son?" (Luke 4:20-22)

But there was a negative reaction when the people realized that He had claimed to be the fulfillment of Isaiah's prophecy and when He rebuked them for their rejection.

> So all those in the synagogue, when they heard these things, were filled with wrath, and rose up and thrust Him out of the city; and they led Him to the brow of the hill on which their city was built, that they might throw Him down over the cliff. Then passing through the midst of them, He went His way (Luke 4:28-30).

What was Jesus to do?

This early synagogue experience was an apparent disaster. Even in His own hometown He was rejected in the synagogue. Perhaps He should seek some other venue. Obviously, synagogues were too tradition bound and closed-minded to accept any different interpretation or revelation.

If Jesus had made that choice, He would have robbed Himself and His disciples of one of the most valuable opportunities for the spread of the gospel.

You see, Jesus knew about synagogues. They were locally owned and locally controlled. They were autonomous and independent, and there was no central authority regulating them. That meant that each one was different. Neither the faults nor the virtues of any one were to be attributed to the others. His experience in one was not an indication of what He might expect in others.

Consequently, we read, "Jesus went about all the cities and villages, teaching in their synagogues, preaching the gospel of the kingdom, and healing every sickness and every disease among the people" (Matthew 9:35).

After the resurrection, the disciples of Jesus preached in the synagogues of Jerusalem (Acts 6). Paul's procedure, wherever he went, was to go first to the synagogue to preach Jesus. In Acts 17:1-2, for example, "Now when they had passed through Amphipolis and Apollonia, they came to

Thessalonica, where there was a synagogue of the Jews. Then Paul, as his custom was, went in to them, and for three Sabbaths reasoned with them from the Scriptures."

Modern Application

The only organization the Lord has authorized for His church is local. Each local assembly is independent and autonomous, and overseen by elders, just as was true of the synagogues. Also, like synagogues, they have no central authority of any kind to direct or regulate their affairs. In New Testament days, a synagogue and a local church were so much alike that James actually used the Greek word, synagogue, to refer to a local assembly of Christians (James 2:2 – usually translated *assembly*).

All of this means that each local church will be different. As said above of synagogues, neither the faults nor the virtues of any one are to be attributed to the others. The seven churches of Asia, described in Revelation 2 and 3, are an example of such variation among churches in New Testament days.

Occasionally, someone who has had what he considers a bad experience with a local church of Christ vows never again to have anything to do with "The Church of Christ." This is as unreasonable as it would have been for Jesus to avoid all synagogues after His experience in Nazareth.

Local congregations are made up of imperfect individuals, so not one is perfect. However, even the weakest ones provide benefits to those who participate in whatever they do that is scriptural. One of the benefits is the assembly in which Christians "consider one another in order to stir up love and good works" (Hebrews 10:24-25). When Saul of Tarsus came to Jerusalem following his conversion, he immediately took steps to "join the disciples" (Acts 9:26). He needed their fellowship.

A young man who desires to "increase in favor with God" should take full advantage of the benefits offered by such a congregation.

1. Here he will find his greatest encouragement as he seeks to "be an example to the believers in word, in conduct, in love, in spirit, in faith, in purity" (1 Timothy 4:12).

2. Here he will have the most opportunity to learn God's word as a supplement to the wonderful advantage he now has in possessing his own copy of the scriptures.

3. Here is where he will most likely have opportunity, especially if he desires it, to exercise himself in godliness by learning to read and pray publicly as well as to begin teaching publicly.

Schools and Bible Camps operated by Christians provide some spiritual benefits to young Christians who "hunger and thirst for righteousness", but not one of these is a substitute for the training organization Jesus designed—the local church.

Some congregations do not provide opportunities for young Christians to the degree that they should. But after all, it was that imperfect synagogue in Nazareth which Jesus had customarily attended on the Sabbath. Take advantage of whatever is available, imperfect though it may be.

Jesus did!

Questions

1. What is the history of synagogues?

2. How did synagogue worship differ from worship in the temple?

3. What opportunities did the synagogue offer devout young Jewish men?

4. How do we know that Jesus attended synagogue regularly when He was growing up in Nazareth?

5. What was the first reaction in the Nazareth synagogue when Jesus returned as a teacher and read from Isaiah 61:1-2 and made comments?

6. What was their second reaction?

7. Did Jesus continue preaching in other synagogues? Why?

8. What use did Paul make of synagogues?

9. How does the New Testament church compare with synagogues in organization?

10. Why is it foolish to reject all churches of Christ because of a bad experience in one?

11. What advantages do local congregations offer a devout young man who wishes to increase his usefulness in the kingdom?

12. Is membership and participation in a local church optional?

Chapter 8

His Affiliations

"...that they all may be one, as You, Father, are in Me, and I in You; that they also may be one in Us" (John 17:21)

The Cambridge Dictionary defines *affiliation* as "a <u>connection</u> with a political party or <u>religion</u>, or with a <u>larger organization</u>."

Affiliation has its appeal. People desire association with organizations for various reasons. Periods of stress cause people to feel lonely and in need of companionship. Such affiliation offers freedom from the necessity of thinking for oneself and an escape from personal responsibility for bad decisions. It provides opportunities for those who desire to be leaders by providing them with sheep who are willing to follow. In association with a party, one can gain a degree of respect which would usually be impossible acting alone. Parties honor their own loyal party members.

There were both religious and political parties in the land where Jesus lived, and He could have become affiliated with any one of them if He had chosen.

Religious Parties

The religious parties are the ones with which Bible students
are most familiar. There were the Pharisees, Sadducees, and
Essenes.

The Pharisees were noted for their emphasis on keeping
the law. Jesus kept the law and taught others of His day to
do so. But He could not accept the traditions which the
Pharisees added to the law. He applied Isaiah 29:13 to them:
"And in vain they worship Me, teaching *as* doctrines the
commandments of men" (Matthew 15:9). So, for this and
other reasons, Jesus could not be a Pharisee.

The Sadducees rejected the traditions of the Pharisees. They
were the party of the priests, and they were much concerned
about the temple. Jesus agreed with them in rejecting the
traditions of the Pharisees, and He was also concerned about
the temple, though He was more concerned with its spiritual
purity than its protection and preservation as a building.
But the Sadducees denied a future resurrection and did not
believe in angels and spirits (Acts 23:8). Jesus believed in all
of these realities, so He could not be a Sadducee.

The Essenes are not mentioned in scripture. As far as we
know, Jesus had no contact with them, nor did many other
people. Their writings, which have been found in abundance,
reveal that they were so concerned for personal purity that
they huddled together in isolated communities and avoided
contact with the outside world. Jesus was equally concerned

for personal purity, but His purpose was to associate with "sinners" so that He might save them. Indeed, one of the most common charges against Him was that He ate and drank with sinners. So, Jesus could not be an Essene.

Does this mean that Jesus was not religious? His religious teaching and practice were perfect. His whole life was pleasing to God. He attended the synagogues, but He did not affiliate with one of the religious parties of His day. To do so would have been an endorsement of the various errors that were to be found in each of them. And membership in any one of them would have limited His independence to criticize and instruct them in changes they needed to make. He was simply a servant of God, doing the will of God and teaching others to do the same.

Jesus did not establish another religious party.

Jesus called lost men and women to come to Him for salvation. Those who accepted His call were more of a family than an institution. He called them His church (Matthew 16:18), but in the language He was speaking, that meant no more than an assembly of people and it did not suggest an institution of any kind. Like an extended family, there were groups living in different cities and they met together for worship and encouragement, but He ordained no human head. He established no headquarters or central office for sending out instructions or receiving reports. He arranged for His message to be written by His apostles and prophets but authorized no successors to add to it. He set up no legislature

or publishing house to disseminate authoritative decrees or
to provide official interpretation of the message that He
had authorized. And He set up no hierarchy of ascending
importance. His arrangement was: "you are all brethren"
(Matthew 23:8), again reminiscent of a family where all
members are equal.

There are numerous religious organizations (usually called
denominations) in our world, many of them claiming to
follow Jesus. They attract as many people as possible to join
their churches. Like the parties of Jesus' day, they all have
some good about them, but all of them practice and teach
things that Jesus did not authorize. The same reasons that
prevented Jesus from affiliating with the parties of His day
are valid reasons for us to avoid affiliation with those of our
day.

Some who consider themselves members of the "one true
church" are, in their minds affiliated with a network of
churches known as Churches of Christ. "Church of Christ" is
a scriptural designation for any one of those local assemblies
described in the New Testament. But if one thinks of those
words as describing a unit of an association or network
known as "The Church of Christ," to that person it becomes
a denomination. Such an association or network may even
lack designated headquarters and a recognized hierarchy, but
if good standing requires accepting traditional "church of
Christ doctrine" and defending "church of Christ practices"
then affiliation is to be avoided. The church that Jesus
established was composed of saved individuals and was not

a worldwide institution whose membership or congregations could be numbered along with its colleges, hospitals, orphanages, etc. That's something totally different.

Even among those who attempt to be "Christians only", parties may form around a prominent preacher, around a religious paper or school or even around some peculiar interpretation of scripture. Whenever an individual is influenced in his convictions by concern for his standing "in the brotherhood" he is affiliated with a party. And whenever, among Christians, there develops an "us and them" distinction, a party has been formed.

Even today, one can be just a Christian without affiliating with any denomination or party. Membership in a local church is encouraged in scripture so long as one can be involved without compromising what he sees to be the Lord's will for him. But loyalty must always be to Christ, not even to the local church. Churches are made up of people, and people can leave the Lord.

Political Parties

There were also political parties in the days of Jesus.

The Herodians were strong supporters of the Roman government and of Herod who was its local representative. Some went so far as to suggest that Herod the Great might be the Messiah. In harmony with their loyalty to Rome, they insisted that Jews should pay taxes to Rome.

The Zealots were on the other end of the political spectrum. They were so violently opposed to the Romans that they engaged in secret violence, carrying short, concealed weapons with which to murder Roman officials as opportunity was afforded.

With which party did Jesus affiliate Himself? The answer, of course, is none. As was true of the religious parties, each political party stood for ideas and practices that were contrary to the truth that Jesus taught. His affiliation with either party would have been an endorsement of things contrary to His convictions and would have compromised His influence.

Interestingly enough, the Pharisees who did not believe in paying taxes to Rome, joined with their opponents, the Herodians, to try to trap their common enemy, Jesus.

They sent to Him their disciples with the Herodians, saying, "Teacher, we know that You are true, and teach the way of God in truth; nor do You care about anyone, for You do not regard the person of men. Tell us, therefore, what do You think? Is it lawful to pay taxes to Caesar, or not" (Matthew 22:16-17)?

They thought they had Him. If He sided with the Herodians and said, "Pay taxes," He would lose the respect of the majority of the people who opposed the taxation. On the other hand, if He stood with the Pharisees and said, "Do not pay taxes," the Herodians would report Him to the Roman officials, and He would be accused of insurrection. With which group would He stand, the Pharisees or the Herodians?

His answer, after examining a Roman coin that contained the image of Caesar: "Render therefore to Caesar the things that are Caesar's, and to God the things that are God's" (Matthew 22:21).

Which party did He always side with? The answer is obvious - with none of them. Just like the religious parties, the political parties may be right on some things, but most support wrong and ungodly positions on some issues.

Before identifying with any party, a Christian who is determined to follow Jesus will ask, "Am I ready to give my endorsement to this party and to all it stands for?" Would Jesus do so if He were on earth today? Will my influence in support of my convictions be stronger with or without joining a party?

What party of Jesus's day, religious or political, did as much for His nation as He did, working simply on His own as a dedicated servant of God?

Questions

1. What is the meaning of *affiliation*?

2. What are some reasons that membership in an organization is appealing?   What are some dangers in such membership?

3. What religious parties existed when Jesus was on earth?

4. Did Jesus agree with each religious party on at least one issue?   Why did He not join a religious party?

5. What is a denomination
    Why would it be wrong to join one?

6. How many saved people are in the church that Jesus established?

    Is it an association or network of local congregations that can be counted and listed in an official directory?

    Must individuals be loyal to traditions established by agreement among such a network of congregations?

    What alone determines the official doctrine and practice that one should follow?

7. What were some of the political parties in the land when Jesus lived?

8. Did Jesus join one?

9. Did Jesus encourage obedience and payment of taxes to the government?

10. Can identification with a political party begin to overshadow our identification with Christ's kingdom?
    What might be some indications that such is happening in our hearts?

Chapter 9

His Race

*"Whoever does the will of God is My brother and My sister
and mother" (Mark 3:35).*

When I lived and preached in West Africa, it
was common for someone to ask, "Why was
Jesus born white?"

Jesus had to be born with some color. If He
had been born black, the question would have been, "Why
was Jesus born black?" There is no evidence anywhere that
He considered His color of any significance. That will be the
attitude of those who are like Him.

Some significant facts:

1. Jesus was not born white. He was not Caucasian, a term
generally considered synonymous with white. He was not
a descendant of Japheth from whom most Europeans are
descended. No credibility is to be attached to the paintings
that show Him with a very white complexion; this is but the
imagination of the painter.

2. Jesus was not born black. Most will agree that this is true.

3. Jesus was descended from Noah's son, Shem. Shem's descendants became the Semitic peoples who settled parts of the Arabian Peninsula, including what is now Saudi Arabia, Yemen, Jordan, Israel, and Lebanon. Their usual color was neither black nor white, but dark. This was likely the color of our Lord's complexion.

4. Jesus claimed relationship with all "who do the will of God" regardless of color. "Whoever does the will of God is My brother and My sister and mother" (Mark 3:35).

Jesus was no racist! Like all of us, He was born belonging to a particular race, but that did not make Him a racist. Even the Pharisees testified, though facetiously, "You are not partial to anyone" (Matthew 22:16 *NASB*). Though He spent most of His life surrounded by Jews, He treated with equal respect the Gentiles with whom He had contact.

Jesus healed the servant of a Roman Centurion (Matthew 4:5-13) who was not a Jew, and He commended His faith as being greater than that of any Jews He had met, saying, "Assuredly, I say to you, I have not found such great faith, not even in Israel" (verse 10)!

Jesus cast a demon from the daughter of a Syro-Phoenician woman who was most likely a Canaanite and a descendant of Ham (Matthew 15:21-28). And He commended her faith as well, saying. "O woman, great is your faith" (verse 28).

Faith is what Jesus was seeking, and the race of one who possessed it made no difference. During His lifetime, He was conscious of those who were not Jews whom He intended to bring into His fold. "Other sheep I have which are not of this fold; them also I must bring, and they will hear My voice; and there will be one flock *and* one shepherd" (John 10:17).

After His resurrection, He instructed "that repentance and remission of sins should be preached in His name to all nations" (Luke 24:37), and to "every creature" (Mark 16:15). He commissioned His disciples to be His witnesses "in Jerusalem, and in all Judea and Samaria, and to the end of the earth" (Acts 1:8).

After His ascension and Pentecost, He made special arrangements for an Ethiopian from Africa to hear the gospel (Acts 8). And He made a special appearance to Saul of Tarsus, explaining that "he is a chosen vessel of Mine to bear My name before Gentiles, kings, and the children of Israel (Acts 9:15).

When Peter, due to prejudice, was still unprepared to preach to Gentiles, he was given a rather puzzling heavenly vision. At first, he did not understand it, but subsequent events revealed its meaning. He said, "God has shown me that I should not call any man common or unclean…In truth I perceive that God shows no partiality. But in every nation whoever fears Him and works righteousness is accepted by Him" (Acts 10:28, 34-35).

The saints in heaven praise the Lamb, saying

> You were slain,
> And have redeemed us to God by Your blood
> Out of every tribe and tongue and people and nation
> (Revelation 5:9).

If there is no racial distinction in heaven, how can it be defended among God's saints on earth?

All of this was fulfillment of God's promise to Abraham: "In your seed all the nations of the earth shall be blessed" (Genesis 22:18). Jesus was the "seed of Abraham" (Galatians 3:16). "And the Scripture, foreseeing that God would justify the Gentiles by faith, preached the gospel to Abraham beforehand, *saying,* 'In you all the nations shall be blessed'" (Galatians 3:8).

In Christ, there is no place for racial pride!

Even Saul of Tarsus had to be changed before He could "bear [Christ's] name before the Gentiles." Before his conversion he took great pride in his racial background. Philippians 3:5 reads like a proud recitation of racial identity. "Circumcised the eighth day, of the stock of Israel, *of* the tribe of Benjamin, a Hebrew of the Hebrews; concerning the law, a Pharisee."

But notice the change which he next reports that took place in his conversion.

But what things were gain to me, these I have counted
loss for Christ. Yet indeed I also count all things loss for
the excellence of the knowledge of Christ Jesus my Lord,
for whom I have suffered the loss of all things, and count
them as rubbish, that I may gain Christ. (Philippians 3:7-8)

When Paul was baptized into Christ (Romans 6:3), he lost
sight of all racial distinction. He could write to the Gentile
Christians in Galatia,

> For you are all sons of God through faith in Christ
> Jesus. For as many of you as were baptized into Christ have
> put on Christ. There is neither Jew nor Greek, there is
> neither slave nor free, there is neither male nor female; for
> you are all one in Christ Jesus. (Galatians 3:26-28)

Racial consciousness seems to be a special characteristic of
our times. Propaganda through numerous media is designed
to inflame it. Each race seems to be competing for a claim to
superiority, even though the expressed appeal is for equality.
Such competition leads to tension among races that too often
turns into violence. Sadly, such racial sensitivity is sometimes
found among Christians.

> But now you yourselves are to put off all these: anger,
> wrath, malice, blasphemy, filthy language out of your
> mouth. Do not lie to one another, since you have put
> off the old man with his deeds, and have put on the
> new *man* who is renewed in knowledge according to
> the image of Him who created him, where there is

neither Greek nor Jew, circumcised nor uncircumcised,
barbarian, Scythian, slave *nor* free, but Christ *is* all and in all
(Colossians 3:8-11).

This old hymn by John Oxenham may have some language
that seems strange, but read it and understand its message.

> In Christ there is no east or west,
> In him no south or north;
> But one great family bound by love
> Throughout the whole wide earth.
>
> Join hands, disciples in the faith,
> Whate'er your race may be!
> Who serve each other in Christ's love
> Are surely kin to me.
>
> In Christ now meet both east and west,
> In him meet south and north;
> All Christlike souls are one in him,
> Throughout the whole wide earth.

Questions

1. What does the Bible say about the color of Jesus skin?
What does this indicate about it?

2. Whom did Jesus claim as His "brother, sister and mother?"

3. List some examples of Jesus commending those of other races.

4. Among whom did He instruct His disciples to preach "repentance and remission of sins"?

5. To whom was Saul of Tarsus called to preach?

6. What did Peter learn about God from his strange heavenly vision (Acts 10:28, 34-35)?

7. According to the saints in heaven, whom did Jesus redeem by His blood?

8. Whom did God say would be blest through Abraham's seed?

9. What change did Paul have to make in the things of which he boasted?

10. What does Galatians 3:26-27 teach us about racial distinctions "in Christ"?

Chapter 10

His Prayers

"He went out to the mountain to pray,
and continued all night" (Luke 6:12).

Anyone who determines to follow the example of Jesus in his life will often have occasion to ask, "What would Jesus do?" This question became so popular a few years ago that the letters WWJD were to be seen often on pins, banners, T-shirts and elsewhere. It is a good question to ask.

However, asking the question does not always guarantee a right response. Often the person asking the question does not know what Jesus would do. At other times, one may know but not have the wisdom or courage to do what Jesus would do.

Of course, a variety of correct answers could be given to this question, depending on the circumstances. However, scanning only the book of Luke, there is one answer that would recur again and again.

What would Jesus do...

When entering His life's work?

When all the people were baptized, it came to pass that Jesus also was baptized; and while He prayed, the heaven was opened (Luke 4:21).

When pressed by crowds?

However, the report went around concerning Him all the more; and great multitudes came together to hear, and to be healed by Him of their infirmities. So He Himself often withdrew into the wilderness and prayed (Luke 5:15-16).

When choosing His future helpers?

Now it came to pass in those days that He went out to the mountain to pray, and continued all night in prayer to God. And when it was day, He called His disciples to Himself; and from them He chose twelve whom He also named apostles (Luke 6:12-13).

When preparing to make a shocking announcement?

And it happened, as He was alone praying, that His disciples joined Him and He [spoke to] them...saying, the Son of Man must suffer many things, and be rejected by the elders and chief priests and scribes, and be killed, and be raised the third day" (Luke 9:18,22).

When contemplating death?

As He prayed, the appearance of His face was altered, and His robe became white and glistening. And behold, two men talked with Him, who were Moses and Elijah, who appeared in glory and spoke of His decease which He was about to accomplish at Jerusalem (Luke 9:29-31).

When learning of success of a preaching tour.

Then the seventy returned with joy, saying, "Lord, even the demons are subject to us in Your name... In that hour Jesus rejoiced in the Spirit and said, "I thank You, Father, Lord of heaven and earth, that You have hidden these things from the wise and prudent and revealed them to babes. Even so, Father, for so it seemed good in Your sight" (Luke 10:17,21).

When a friend is facing temptation?

And the Lord said, 'Simon, Simon! Indeed, Satan has asked for you, that he may sift you as wheat. But I have prayed for you, that your faith should not fail' (Luke 22:31-32).

When awaiting arrest and execution?

And He was withdrawn from them about a stone's throw, and He knelt down and prayed, saying, "Father, if it is Your will, take this cup away from Me; nevertheless not My will, but Yours, be done" (Luke 22:41-42).

When being painfully mistreated?

Then Jesus said, "Father, forgive them, for they do not know what they do (Luke 22:34).

When dying?

And when Jesus had cried out with a loud voice, He said, "Father, into Your hands I commit My spirit.' Having said this, He breathed His last" (Luke 23:46).

We may not always know what decision Jesus would make when we are faced with a complicated question, but one thing we can be sure of—He would pray! And this is something we all can do. Doubtless, a humble and sincere prayer, coupled with a knowledge of Jesus's teaching, will make much more likely the kind of godly decision that Jesus would make.

"Lord, teach us to pray"

"Now it came to pass, as He was praying in a certain place, when He ceased, that one of His disciples said to Him, "Lord, teach us to pray, as John also taught his disciples" (Luke 11:1).

The disciples had doubtless been hearing prayers all their lives, but when they heard Jesus pray it was something different. No wonder they asked Him to teach them to pray. We can surely use the same lesson. Thankfully, it is recorded.

So He said to them, "When you pray, say:

Our Father in heaven,
Hallowed be Your name.
Your kingdom come.
Your will be done
On earth as it is in heaven.
Give us day by day our daily bread.
And forgive us our sins,
For we also forgive everyone who is indebted to us.
And do not lead us into temptation,
But deliver us from the evil one" (Luke 11:3-4).

This prayer is slightly different from the version found in Matthew 6:9-13. This is evidence that they are not to be memorized and repeated word for word; which one should we choose? They are enough alike, however, to be a model for us. A master carpenter might show his apprentice how to make a table, saying, "When you make a table make it like this." That does not mean that every table the apprentice makes will have the same shape, size, and appearance as the one he is shown. But even the last one he makes in his lifetime may be slightly influenced by that model he saw his master make.

This model prayer should be an encouragement to one who is just beginning to lead public prayers. First, your prayers do not have to be long; this one is short. Your prayers do not have to include many big and impressive words; this one does not. Your prayers are not to be prayed to people but to God (Matthew 6:5-8).

This prayer does contain some characteristics which are appropriate for all prayers:

1. An address: "Our Father in heaven".

2. Praise: "Hallowed be Your name."

3. A Kingdom petition: "Your kingdom come. Your will be done on earth as *it is* in heaven."

4. A petition for physical needs: "Give us day by day our daily bread."

5. A petition for spiritual needs: "And forgive us our sins, for we also forgive everyone who is indebted to us. And do not lead us into temptation, but deliver us from the evil one'"

Nowhere in the New Testament do we read of anyone's praying this exact prayer word for word. Some recorded prayers do not contain all of these elements, while many prayers also include thanksgiving. The main ingredient of an acceptable prayer is humble sincerity. This was the quality that was evident in a prayer to which Jesus gave His specific approval. It consisted of only seven words: "God, be merciful to me a sinner" (Luke 18:13).

But how could Jesus pray all night? Prayer is more than a list of requests. Prayer is talking to God.

Be anxious for nothing, but in everything by prayer and supplication, with thanksgiving, let your requests be made known to God; and the peace of God, which surpasses all understanding, will guard your hearts and minds through Christ Jesus (Philippians 4:6-7).

We can talk to God concerning anything about which we are anxious. We can ask Him for anything we need, and then thank Him for all He has done for us. As we practice prayer and as our faith in God grows stronger, we will find our prayers growing longer. But longer prayers are only fitting for private prayers. It was only in private that Jesus prayed all night.

One is not ready to pray in public until he has learned to pray in secret. So many of the prayers of Jesus were private prayers which no one heard but God. Jesus taught His disciples the importance of secret prayer.

> But you, when you pray, go into your room, and when you have shut your door, pray to your Father who *is* in the secret *place;* and your Father who sees in secret will reward you openly (Matthew 6:6).

Prayer will be an important element in the life of anyone who would be like Jesus

> Who, in the days of His flesh, when He had offered up prayers and supplications, with vehement cries and tears to Him who was able to save Him from death, and was heard because of His godly fear (Hebrews 5:7).

Questions

1. Is "What would Jesus do" a good question for us to ask about any decision?

2. Why does asking the question sometimes fail to lead us to do the right thing?

3. What must be coupled with prayer if we are to assure wise decisions?

4. What did Jesus do in connection with every major decision or action of His life?

5. What did the disciples request when they heard Jesus pray?

6. What evidence can you cite to suggest that this is not a prayer to be memorized and repeated verbatim?

7. What is the longest word in the English translation of the prayer Jesus taught?

8. If we take the prayer Jesus taught as a model, what effect will it have on our prayers?

9. If we learn how to pray from this prayer what kind of requests will dominate, physical or spiritual?

10. Why do you think Jesus approved of the prayer that He commended in Luke 18:13?

11. Why do you think Jesus was able to pray all night?

12. Who should be foremost in our minds when we pray? What makes this difficult in leading public prayer?

Discussion Question

Discuss some differences between public prayers and private prayers.

His Association with Women

Chapter 11

His Association with Women

And the twelve were with Him, and certain women" (Luke 8:1-2).

Headlines in recent years have been filled with reports of prominent men of the world whose mistreatment of women has been uncovered. The misconduct of heroic historical figures, which for years has been concealed, has also been revealed. More shocking is the evidence that nationally known religious leaders have also been guilty. Even some Old Testament heroes like David sinned grievously in their relationship with women.

During His lifetime, Jesus was associated with many women. Some, like His mother, were outstandingly pure when He first met them. Some had a sordid background, yet His life was completely free of the slightest hint of indiscretion. Nor do we read of any indiscretion in any of the disciples with whom He was associated. There must be a reason for this.

Perhaps the reason is found in the Old Testament. Do you remember what Samuel learned about God's view of human beings? "The Lord said to Samuel, 'Do not look at his appearance or at his physical stature…For the Lord does not see as man sees; for man looks at the outward appearance, but the Lord looks at the heart."

Jesus Looked at the Heart

Jesus looked at the heart of those He met, whether men or women, and He evaluated them on the basis of what they were thinking and what they could become.

One of the greatest mistakes that men can make is judging women primarily by their outward appearance. The wickedness of Noah's day is explained in part in Genesis 6:3. "The sons of God saw the daughters of men, that they were beautiful; and they took wives for themselves of all whom they chose." The "daughters of men" were apparently the wicked descendants of Cain.

Jacob loved Rachel more than Leah because "Leah's eyes were delicate, but Rachel was beautiful of form and appearance" (Genesis 29:17). Yet, Leah proved to be the better woman.

Besides the sin of lusting that is inherent in pornography, men who engage in it begin to judge every woman by her outward form and to be attracted by seductive conduct. Young men seeking wives often pass up the best possible choices because they do not fit the picture they have come to idolize. Married men make unfavorable comparisons

between the women they see on their screens and their godly
wives. Pornography before and after marriage is one of the
most destructive factors in failed marriages. The women
of pornography are the modern equivalent of the immoral
woman that Solomon described in the Proverbs with the
warning:

> Pay attention to the words of my mouth:
> Do not let your heart turn aside to her ways,
> Do not stray into her paths;
> For she has cast down many wounded,
> And all who were slain by her were strong men.
> Her house is the way to hell,
> Descending to the chambers of death. (Proverbs 7:24-27)

It was the immoral women of Moab who enticed the men
of Israel to join in the sensuous worship of their fertility
god. God punished Israel with a plague that took the lives
of 24,000 Israelites, and He ordered a war which resulted in
the death of all the women who had been guilty (Numbers
31:1-18). God's wrath against such women and their victims
is not expressed immediately today as it was then, but it is
certain in eternity both for such women as well as for those
who are enticed by them. Anyone who is already enslaved to
pornography should repent and seek help from a godly friend
who will help him to overcome his addiction.

Jesus, of course, had a miraculous ability that we do not
have to see inside the mind of those He met. "He knew
all men, and had no need that anyone should testify of man,

for He knew what was in man" (John 2:24-25). But even we are not left to guess about the heart of women with whom we come in contact.

We can judge them by the emphasis that is evident in their preparations to appear in public. Rather than spending excessive time before the mirror, the greater concern of the godly woman is to beautify "the hidden person of the heart, with the incorruptible beauty of a gentle and quiet spirit, which is very precious in the sight of God" (1 Peter 3:4).

Godly women are careful to adorn themselves with "modest apparel, with propriety and moderation, not with braided hair or gold or pearls or costly clothing, but, which is proper for women professing godliness, with good works" (1 Timothy 2:9-10). They do not neglect their appearance completely, but they prefer that those who meet them remember them more for their character than their looks.

Godly women will not be found in bars and places of worldly amusement, but in the company of other godly women such as those who accompanied Jesus. They will be found where the saints assemble. They will be 'hungry and thirsty for righteousness" rather than for gossip, publicity, and approval of the world. You will find them ready to read the Bible and pray with you.

Above all things, they will encourage you to be pure in your thoughts and actions and will never do anything calculated to "lead you on" toward sensuality and lustful conduct.

No, Christlike men are not limited in their ability to find godly female companions if that is what they are seeking.

Jesus Respected Women

The respect that Jesus had for women is evident first in His relationship with His mother. Even in His teen years, He was subject to His parents, which would include Mary (Luke 2:51). The way He addressed His mother sometime seems a little too formal in today's language, but it was the language of respect in His time. He did not allow His mother to determine His timing for doing God's work at the wedding feast (John 2:1-4), and He did not allow her and His brothers to interfere with His ministry in Capernaum (Mark 3:21, 31-35). Yet, even when He was dying, He was mindful of her need for care and entrusted her to the "the disciple whom He loved" (John 19:26-27). Little wonder she was among the 120 disciples who were gathered in Jerusalem following His ascension, waiting for the coming of the Holy Spirit Whom He had promised (Acts 1:14).

Dwight M. Pratt in International Standard Bible Encyclopedia (1946 Ed., Vol 5, p. 3104) gives an excellent summary of the pure relationship that Jesus had with women.

> Women in all ranks of society found in Him a benefactor and friend, before unknown in all the history of their sex. They accompanied Him, with the twelve, in His preaching tours from city to city, some, like Mary Magdalene, grateful because healed from their moral infirmities (Luke 8:2),

others, like Joanna the wife of Chuza, and Susanna, to minister to His needs (Luke 8:3). Even those who were ostracized from society were recognized by Him, on the basis of immortal values, and restored to a womanhood of virtue and Christian devotion (Luke 7:37-50). Mothers had occasions to rejoice in His blessing their children (Mark 10:13-16); and in His raising their dead (Luke 7:12-15). Women followed Him on His last journey from Galilee to Jerusalem, ministered to Him on His way to Calvary (Matthew 27:55-56); witnessed His crucifixion (Luke 23:49); accompanied His body to the sepulcher (Matthew 27:61); prepared spices and ointment for His burial (Luke 23:56); were first at the tomb on the morning of His resurrection (Matthew 28:1); and were the first to whom the risen Lord appeared (Mark 16:9)....Women had the honor of being the first to announce the fact of the resurrection to the chosen disciples (Luke 24:9-10, 22).

Jesus is an example for all men in the treatment of women. Paul encouraged Timothy, "Exhort...older women as mothers, younger women as sisters, with all purity" (1 Timothy 5:2).

Under guidance of the Holy Spirit, Paul revealed some restrictions on the service that women are to render in a public way (1 Corinthians 14:34). Guided by the same Spirit, he wrote: "Let a woman learn in silence with all submission. And I do not permit a woman to teach or to have authority over a man, but to be in silence" (1 Timothy 2:11-12). Some have undertaken to set Paul against Jesus.

However, it should be noted that Jesus did not appoint a woman among His apostles, nor did He ever encourage a woman to do anything that would have violated the inspired teaching of Paul.

Jesus Gave Husbands an Example

Jesus never married. Yet, in the Ephesian letter, valuable lessons for husbands are drawn from His relationship with the church.

> Husbands, love your wives, just as Christ also loved the church and gave Himself for her, that He might sanctify and cleanse her with the washing of water by the word, that He might present her to Himself a glorious church, not having spot or wrinkle or any such thing, but that she should be holy and without blemish. So husbands ought to love their own wives as their own bodies; he who loves his wife loves himself. For no one ever hated his own flesh, but nourishes and cherishes it, just as the Lord does the church. For we are members of His body, of His flesh and of His bones. "For this reason a man shall leave his father and mother and be joined to his wife, and the two shall become one flesh." (Ephesians 5:25-31)

A full discussion of this text is not possible here. However, we can note several very important facts that it reveals.

1. Husbands are to love their wives as Christ loved the church.

2. He loved the church enough that He was willing to die for her.

3. He did not enter His relationship with the church for what He would gain, but for what He could give.

4. His goal in marriage was to sanctify and cleanse the church—to make her better in her relationship with God.

5. His reward would be to present her to Himself, spiritually glorified "without spot or wrinkle or any such thing."

6. Husbands should love their wives as they love themselves.

7. Husbands should "nourish and cherish" their wives as they do their own bodies.

If a husband chooses a wife on the basis of her "inner beauty" rather than her mere appearance, and if He treats her as Christ has treated the church, he can expect increasing loyalty from her. He can also expect a stable marriage in contrast with the fragile relationships among those in the world.

Doubtless, it was the attitude that Jesus showed toward the women in His life and the respect with which He treated them that accounted for their loyalty to Him.

Questions

1. Why do you think Jesus was able to avoid any scandal involving women?

2. What mistake did the descendants of Seth make that contributed to the wickedness of the generation destroyed by the flood (Genesis 6:3)?

3. Why did Jacob love Rachel more than Leah?

4. List two or three dangers of pornography besides the sin of lusting.

5. If one is involved in pornography what should he do promptly?

6. What quality in a woman is "very precious in the sight of God" (1 Peter 3:4)?

7. With what do godly women adorn themselves (1 Timothy 2:9-10)?

8. What influence will a godly woman have on a man when they are alone on a date?

9. How did Jesus show respect for His mother?

10. What are some evidences of the respect good women had for Jesus?

11. What restriction did the Holy Spirit through Paul place on women's public role (1 Timothy 2:12)?

Did Jesus ever encourage a woman to do anything that would have violated Paul's teaching?

Discussion Question

What does the example of Jesus teach husbands about how they should treat their wives?

Chapter 12

His Love

"Greater love has no one than this." *(John 15:13)*

W hat is manliness? Who is the ideal man? Sociologists tell us that the answer will differ with different cultures.

Our own western culture, influenced by popular novels and movies, would probably answer that manliness is best described by the Spanish word *machismo*. This word is defined by the American Heritage Dictionary of the English Language, 5th Edition, as a "sense of manly pride, associated with an attitude that the proper expression of masculinity includes virility, courage, and an entitlement to dominate, especially over women." To some it also means cursing, drinking and promiscuity. It includes an "I don't get mad, I get even" attitude. Given this definition, the ideal man would be someone like John Wayne or Clint Eastwood. This popular view of manliness would judge Jesus a "sissy" and disqualify Him as a model of manhood. He said of Himself, "I am gentle and lowly in heart" (Matthew 11:29). We have seen how He treated women, and the loyalty He earned from them.

Others in our day have rejected this machismo model and replaced it with one that may best be described by the word, *milquetoast*. This is defined by the same dictionary as "One who has a meek, timid, unassertive nature. A timid, unassertive man or boy fearful of confrontation and easily manipulated and dominated." Anyone who has even scanned the four gospels will reject any such description of Jesus.

If either of these has been your idea of the ideal man, it is one of the concepts that you must change if you are to follow Jesus.

If there is one word that could describe Jesus it would be love.

And this should not be surprising. After all, "God is love" (1 John 4:8); and Jesus is God in fleshly form (John 1:11,14). But we shall see that the love of Jesus is not the emotional, changeable, and sometimes irrational love that is so popular in our day.

The Love of Jesus

Jesus loved God. His love for God is not recorded so much in words as in deeds. "For this is the love of God, that we keep His commandments" (1 John 5:3). Jesus said, "If you keep my commandments you will abide in My love, just as I have kept My Father's commandments and abide in His love" (John 15:10).

Jesus loved all mankind. His love for all is evident in His willingness to "taste death for everyone" (Hebrews 2:9). Yet His love for all does not mean that all will be saved. His first coming was to "give Himself a ransom for all" (1 Timothy 2:6), but when He comes again, He will be "revealed from heaven with His mighty angels, in flaming fire taking vengeance on those who do not know God, and on those who do not obey the gospel of our Lord Jesus Christ" (2 Thessalonians 1:7-8). He is only "the author of eternal salvation to all who obey Him" (Hebrews 5:9).

Jesus loved His enemies. Even as they crucified Him, Jesus prayed, "Father, forgive them, for they do not know what they do" (Luke 23:34). However, these also had to be obedient to be forgiven. Weeks later, after Jesus' ascension, Peter accused His audience of being the ones who had crucified Jesus (Acts 2:23). When they understood that they had crucified their Messiah, they cried out, "'Men and brethren, what shall we do?' Then Peter said to them, 'Repent, and let every one of you be baptized in the name of Jesus Christ for the remission of sins; and you shall receive the gift of the Holy Spirit'" (Acts 2:37-38). The prayer of Jesus for their forgiveness was only granted when they were offered forgiveness and complied with the conditions stated by the Holy Spirit through Peter.

Jesus had a special love for those who loved Him. "Jesus loved Martha and her sister and Lazarus" (John 11:5) who showed their love for Him by their hospitality and generosity. When He wept at the tomb of Lazarus, His love was so evident that "the Jews said, 'See how He loved him!'" (John 11:36).

Jesus had a special love for His apostles, despite their weaknesses. "Having loved His own who were in the world, He loved them to the end" (John 13:1). Even among the twelve, there were three who were closer to Him than the others: Peter, James, and John. And among those three, John only identifies himself in his gospel as "the disciple whom Jesus loved." Whether Jesus had a special love for John, or if John only perceived it to be that way, is not certain.

It is obvious from the above that the love which Jesus possessed is not the shallow emotional kind of infatuation that so many identify with the word, love. It is rather the kind of attitude that the Holy Spirit described in 1 Corinthians 13. In reading that chapter one could place the name of Jesus in place of the word love and it would still be true. For example,

> "[Jesus] suffers long and is kind; [Jesus] does not envy;
> [Jesus] does not parade [Himself], is not puffed up;
> does not behave rudely, does not seek [His] own, is not
> provoked, thinks no evil; does not rejoice in iniquity,
> but rejoices in the truth (verses 4-6).

The manhood of Jesus did not hinder His verbal expressions of love. He described a chain of love in which He was the significant link. Note the following:

In a prayer to God Jesus said, "You loved Me before the foundation of the world" (John 17:24).

To His disciples He said, "As the Father loved Me, I also have loved you; abide in My love" (John 15:9).

And a few moments later: "This is My commandment, that you love one another as I have loved you" (John 15:12).

Loving as Jesus Loved

It is apparent from this that if we would take Jesus as our model, we must be loving persons.

Above all things, we must love God. When asked what the greatest commandment was, Jesus answered, "You shall love the Lord your God with all your heart, with all your soul, and with all your mind. This is the first and great commandment" (Matthew 22:37-38) And loving God as Jesus did is more than mere talk."For this is the love of God, that we keep His commandments" (1 John 5:3).

Jesus reinforced the second great commandment, "You shall love your neighbor as yourself." Then, in the story of the "Good Samaritan" He defined our neighbor as anyone we may encounter who needs our help (Luke 10:25-37).

We must love Jesus (1 Corinthians 16:22). After Peter had denied Jesus, Jesus wanted him, for his own good, to confess his love. Three times, Jesus asked Peter, "Do you love me?" (John 21:15-17). It is important for us to express our love for Him, both in words and in deeds. He said, "Whoever confesses Me before men, him I will also confess before My Father who is in heaven" (Matthew 10:32). And He also said, "If you love Me, keep My commandments" (John 14:15).

Jesus even commands us to love our enemies, and then describes how we are to express it. "I say to you, love your enemies, bless those who curse you, do good to those who hate you, and pray for those who spitefully use you and persecute you" (Matthew 5:44). We must not, however, join with them in sin to gain their friendship. "And have no fellowship with the unfruitful works of darkness, but rather expose them" (Ephesians 5:11).

Anyone who is like Jesus will love the lost. He came into the world "to seek and to save that which was lost" (Luke 19). The "love of Christ" compelled Paul (2 Corinthians 5:14), and that love made him "a debtor both to Greeks and to barbarians, both to wise and to unwise" to preach the gospel to them. (Romans 1:14). If the love of Christ compels us, we will feel the same sense of debt.

But Jesus desires us to have a special love for brethren. Four times, in His last conversation with His apostles before His death, He admonished them to love one another. He had heard the "dispute among them, about which of them should be considered the greatest" (Luke 22:24), and it must have grieved Him. Even now, He must be grieved

by the prideful disputes that so often disturb the unity of
brethren. At least 19 times in the epistles, these instructions
to love one another are repeated. Jesus even identified this
as the mark of true discipleship: "By this all will know
that you are My disciples, if you have love for one another"
(John 13:35).

A special affection for individual Christians is appropriate.
The apostle John addressed his third epistle to "To the
beloved Gaius, whom I love in truth" (3 John 1:1). While we
are to desire the wellbeing of everyone, "brotherly love" is
our special relationship with brothers and sisters in Christ.

The fact that "God is love" means that all love that flows
from Him is pure. Jesus was God's love perfectly revealed
in human form. As we benefit from His perfect reflection
of God's love to us, we must become a link in the chain and
reflect His kind of love to others. "By this we know love,
because He laid down His life for us. And we also ought
to lay down *our* lives for the brethren" (1 John 3:16).

Questions

1. What are the qualities that the world identifies with
manliness?

2. Who are some men the world considers models of manhood?

3. What reveals the love Jesus had for God?

4. Does the fact that Jesus loves all mankind mean that all will be saved?   Who will be saved?

5. Though Jesus prayed for those who crucified Him, what did they have to do to be forgiven?

6. Was Jesus shy about expressing His love orally?

7. Who are some persons that we are specifically commanded to love?

8. Is it wrong for us to have a special love for some persons? For whom should we have a special personal love?

9. What are some dangers of making worldly people our closest and most loved companions?

10. What are some ways that we as Christians are to express our love for one another?

11. Who is the standard of the love we must have for one another (John 15:12)?

Discussion Questions

What does it mean to love God with all our heart, soul, and mind?

Does the fact that we are to love everyone mean that we must approve or accept the lifestyle of those who rebel against the Lord's standard of morality?

Does love for brethren forbid disciplining them when they sin?

Chapter 13

His Cross and Crown

*"If anyone desires to come after Me, let him deny himself,
and take up his cross daily, and follow Me." Luke 9:23*

In the beginning of this study, we observed the goal that Jesus set for Himself in coming to the world. He said, "I have come down from heaven, not to do my own will but the will of him who sent me" (John 6:38). Many a person has set out declaring this same intention only to forsake it when some sacrifice seemed too great. How far would Jesus go? There could be no greater test of His resolve than the cross.

Without doubt, crucifixion was the cruelest form of capital punishment ever devised. In contrast with modern methods which are designed to limit suffering, crucifixion was designed to maximize the suffering, the pain, the humiliation, and the time that the victim remained alive to endure it.

Yet, Jesus came to earth, knowing that He would be crucified.

Jesus was not unaware of the pain involved. His Spirit through David described it graphically in Psalm 22, long before it was even devised. And Jesus could have escaped it.

Jesus knew where His crucifixion would occur. He Himself said, "it cannot be that a prophet should perish outside of Jerusalem" (Luke 13:33). Obviously, He could have avoided Jerusalem. Yet the last six months of His ministry were spent in a slow but deliberate march toward that city. He informed His disciples, "Behold, we are going up to Jerusalem, and the Son of Man will be betrayed to the chief priests and to the scribes; and they will condemn Him to death" (Matthew 20:18).

He knew the time that His crucifixion would occur. From the very beginning of His ministry, He spoke of it as His "hour". Repeatedly He said, "My hour is not yet come." However, during the last week of His life, He said, "The hour has come...Now My soul is troubled, and what shall I say? 'Father, save Me from this hour'? But for this purpose I came to this hour" (John 12:23,27).

Jesus knew in advance who would betray Him and the place His betrayer had arranged for His arrest. He could have avoided the place if He had chosen to do so. And when the armed soldiers came to take Him, rather than running away, He went out to meet them, boldly identifying Himself as the one they were seeking.

None of this is to say that He did not dread the cross. As He faced arrest, He said to His disciples, "My soul is exceedingly sorrowful, even to death." His humanity longed for escape.

> He went a little farther, and fell on the ground, and prayed that if it were possible, the hour might pass from Him.

And He said, "Abba, Father, all things are possible for You.
Take this cup away from Me…" (Mark 14:34-36).

The Hebrew writer records that He "offered up prayers and
supplications, with vehement cries and tears to Him who was
able to save Him from death" (Hebrews 5:8). Taking up His
cross was not easy.

Why Did Jesus Choose to be Crucified?

At least three reasons may be given for the willingness of
Jesus to go to the cross.

The Father's Will: Remember that He came to earth to
do God's will. Bible students will recognize that the above
quotation of His Garden prayer was not finished. After
pleading that, if possible, He might avoid the cross, He
added, "nevertheless, not what I will, but what You will."
After repeating this prayer three times, it was evident that
God's will required the cross. And that settled it. If it was
God's will, it was His will. And with that confidence, He
courageously left His place of prayer and with no hesitation
went forth to face those who had come to arrest Him.

What He saw Beyond the Cross: He knew that He would rise
again. When He first informed His disciples of His impending
death, He said, "The Son of Man must suffer many things, and
be rejected by the elders and chief priests and scribes, and be
killed, and be raised the third day (Luke 9:22). But there was
more. The hour of His crucifixion was "The hour…for the

Son of Man to be glorified" (John 12:23}. The Hebrew writer explains that He, "for the joy that was set before Him endured the cross, despising the shame, and has sat down at the right hand of the throne of God" (Hebrews 12:2).

His Love for Us: He had us in mind. Early in His ministry He explained, "As Moses lifted up the serpent in the wilderness, even so must the Son of Man be lifted up, that whoever believes in Him should not perish but have eternal life" (John 3:14-15). When anticipating His "hour", He said, "And I, if I am lifted up from the earth, will draw all peoples to Myself." (John 12:32-33). The night of His arrest, He observed, "Greater love has no one than this, than to lay down one's life for his friends" (John 15:13). And after His resurrection,

> Thus it is written, and thus it was necessary for the Christ to suffer and to rise from the dead the third day, and that repentance and remission of sins should be preached in His name to all nations, beginning at Jerusalem (Luke 24:46-47).

We Must Take Up Our Cross

Periodically, the U.S. Marine Corps has advertised, "The Marines are looking for a few good men." They are not looking for just any men, but for "good men"—men who are strong, patriotic, loyal and dependable. Not everyone qualifies. They are more concerned with quality than with quantity.

Jesus is looking for good souls who are willing to follow Him even to the cross. Not everyone will qualify. In fact, He said,

"Whoever does not bear his cross and come after Me cannot be My disciple" (Luke 14:27).

Many considered following Jesus but turned back when their cross appeared. A rich young ruler came, asking what He needed to do to inherit eternal life. Jesus saw that his riches were his god, so He said to him,

> One thing you lack: Go your way, sell whatever you have and give to the poor, and you will have treasure in heaven; and come, take up the cross, and follow Me. But he was sad at this word, and went away sorrowful, for he had great possessions" (Mark 10:21-22).

He was not willing to crucify his love of money to follow Jesus. And Jesus let him leave.

What does it mean to take up our cross?

It is common to hear people speak of a physical handicap or sickness as "my cross." Others think of poverty or the death of a loved one as the cross they must bear. However, these are not the cross Jesus referred to. These are hardships about which people have no choice. Taking up the cross of Jesus is something we must choose to do.

When Jesus went out "bearing His cross", He was on His way to Golgotha to be crucified. Taking up our cross indicates a readiness to sacrifice ourselves and whatever may be necessary, even those things that are dearest to us, to follow

Jesus. And it is not just a one-time commitment; it is a daily resolve.

We are taking up our cross when we abandon our old life of sin and begin to let Christ rule us. Paul said, "I have been crucified with Christ; it is no longer I who live, but Christ lives in me; and the life which I now live in the flesh I live by faith in the Son of God…" (Galatians 2:20).

Bearing the cross means being willing to be alienated from our earthly family.

> He who loves father or mother more than Me is not worthy of Me. And he who loves son or daughter more than Me is not worthy of Me. And he who does not take his cross and follow after Me is not worthy of Me" (Matthew 10:37-38).

"And those who are Christ's have crucified the flesh with its passions and desires" (Galatians 5:24). We are crucifying the flesh when we refuse to commit a sin that would feel good, make us popular or provide for us something that we want,

We are taking up our cross when we force ourselves, even against our will, to do something simply because it is God's will.

Why would anyone volunteer for crucifixion?

We have seen the reasons Jesus took up His cross and the same reasons are good enough for us.

The Father's Will: If God's will is our will, then we must sacrifice our bodies to God.

> I beseech you therefore, brethren, by the mercies of God, that you present your bodies a living sacrifice, holy, acceptable to God, which is your reasonable service. And do not be conformed to this world, but be transformed by the renewing of your mind, that you may prove [live out] what is that good and acceptable and perfect will of God (Romans 12:1-2).

What Lies Beyond the Cross:

> For I consider that the sufferings of this present time are not worthy to be compared with the glory which shall be revealed in us" (Romans 8:18). "For our light affliction, which is but for a moment, is working for us a far more exceeding and eternal weight of glory (2 Corinthians 4:17).

"Therefore, my beloved brethren, be steadfast, immovable, always abounding in the work of the Lord, knowing that your labor is not in vain in the Lord" (1 Corinthians 15:58). We are "joint heirs with Christ, if indeed we suffer with Him, that we may also be glorified together" (Romans 8:17).

Our Love for Him: Once we begin to comprehend the undeserved love that Jesus expressed for us, there will be no limit to what will be willing to sacrifice for Him. Paul's reason for crucifying himself was that the Son of God "loved me and gave Himself for me" (Galatians 2:20). Elsewhere, Paul explained: "For the love of Christ compels us, because we judge thus: that if One died for all, then all died; and He died for all, that those who live should live no longer for themselves, but for Him who died for them and rose again" (2 Corinthians 5:14-15).

Conclusion

Following Jesus has always meant taking up His cross. However, bearing His cross may become more difficult in the near future. Laws being made in our world are increasingly protective of various immoral practices and those who oppose those practices are facing progressively serious penalties. In its Dare to Stand publication of March 4, 2022, Family Research Council reported:

> In Finland, a member of parliament, Paivi Rasanen, is currently being tried in court for violating the country's "hate speech" laws. She is being accused of "ethnic agitation" for tweeting a picture of the Bible opened to Romans 1:24-27 in response to her church denomination's choice to participate in a local LGBT pride parade in 2019. If found guilty of these charges, she could end up spending two years in jail or pay a hefty fine. Despite the possible consequences, Paivi Rasanen is standing strong for biblical truth. She has not and will not recant her affirmation of what God's Word says about marriage.

You may already be suffering some alienations for your opposition to the immorality in our society, but true disciples need to be prepared for greater penalties that most likely lie ahead. The time may come in our own country when even scripture quotation may be labeled "hate speech."

Jesus did not hide the consequences of following Him. Rather, He pronounced a blessing on those who were willing to endure them.

> Blessed are those who are persecuted for righteousness' sake, For theirs is the kingdom of heaven. Blessed are you when they revile and persecute you, and say all kinds of evil against you falsely for My sake. Rejoice and be exceedingly glad, for great is your reward in heaven, for so they persecuted the prophets who were before you (Matthew 5:10-12).

Are you willing to take up your cross and follow Jesus?

> Must Jesus bear the cross alone,
> And all the world go free?
> No, there's a cross for everyone,
> And there's a cross for me.
>
> The consecrated cross I'll bear
> Till death shall set me free;
> And then go home my crown to wear,
> For there's a crown for me.
> --Thomas Shepherd

Questions

1. What were some things that made crucifixion such a cruel form of capital punishment?

2. What are some things that Jesus knew in advance about His own crucifixion?

3. What reveals to us that He dreaded it?

4. List at least three reasons why Jesus was willing to be crucified.

   a.

   b.

   c.

5. Why do physical handicaps, poverty, sickness, etc. not qualify as the cross to be taken up?

6. How does Romans 12:1-2 describe cross bearing?

7. What good things lie beyond our cross for us?

8. Why was Paul willing to be "crucified with Christ"?

9. List some individuals who rejected Jesus because they were not willing to take up their cross.

10. Does the rich young ruler have his riches now?
After 2,000 years, do the apostles have their reward for taking up their cross and following Jesus?

11. What is your decision about taking up your cross and following Jesus?

Discussion Questions

What are some things we may have to sacrifice to take up our cross and follow Jesus?

Are there any benefits to be gained by following Jesus in this life?

Are you willing to take up your cross and follow Jesus?

Made in the USA
Middletown, DE
08 July 2022